D0497891

MOSES ON
MANAGEMENT

To Tilley,
with warmest
regards and best wishes

MOSES
ON MANAGEMENT

50 Leadership Lessons from
the Greatest Manager
of All Time

DAVID BARON
with LYNETTE PADWA

POCKET BOOKS
NEW YORK   LONDON   TORONTO   SYDNEY   TOKYO   SINGAPORE

POCKET BOOKS, a division of Simon & Schuster Inc.
1230 Avenue of the Americas, New York, NY 10020

ISBN: 0-671-03259-3

First Pocket Books hardcover printing October 1999

10 9 8 7 6 5 4 3 2 1

Book design by Laura Lindgren and Celia Fuller

Printed in the U.S.A.

To my son,
Jonathan Radner Baron,
and our next generation of leaders

CONTENTS

⬦ *Part Two* ⬦
LEADING IN THE WILDERNESS

✦ *Part Three* ✦
LIVING BY THE CODE

✦ ix ✦

PREFACE

THE GREATEST MANAGER OF ALL TIME. IT'S A BOLD CLAIM, but few would deny that Moses deserves it. With God's help, he bested the mighty Egyptian pharaoh, bringing six-hundred-thousand slaves out of bondage and into nationhood. His laws, created during the forty years he and the Israelites spent in the wilderness, provide the ethical foundation for Judaism, Islam, and Christianity. Yet if Moses were to submit his preliminary résumé today, not even a seasoned headhunter would be able to get him a job. Imagine hiring a manager whose profile reads:

- reluctant to lead
- a stutterer
- distant
- prone to long mountaintop vigils
- temperamental to the point of smashing corporate-mission statements
- strikes out instead of speaking
- settles disputes through swift, violent means
- never reaches his ultimate objective

From our knowledge of him through the Bible and popular culture, Moses seems to be a bundle of contradictions. Is he the resistant, moody shepherd of Exodus or the godlike liberator portrayed by Charlton Heston in *The Ten Commandments?* One moment he's begging the Lord to choose someone else for the job, the next he's striding through the Red Sea like Zeus. The Bible paints a portrait of a flawed and often frustrated leader whose compassion for his people is frequently at odds with his commitment to the Lord. By any account, Moses was a highly complex individual who operated in a wildly uncertain world. For that very reason, his story provides us with insights and leadership tools that are invaluable today.

Every aspect of modern life—from its ethical murkiness to its uncertainty and cynicism—existed tenfold in Moses' day. We may be unsure about our moral compass, but Moses had to *invent* a moral compass. We may face difficult management objectives, but Moses had to lead the sullen and helpless Israelites through an uncharted wilderness, urging them on to a "promised" land. His mission evolved along the way as he realized the breadth of his task: to transform a group of despairing ex-slaves into a nation of optimistic freedom fighters. Now *that* is a paradigm shift.

Moses is revered as a liberator, lawgiver, and intercessor par excellence, but few casual readers of the Bible notice the important leadership lessons that can be gleaned from his story. This book attempts to bring some of these lessons to life. The biblical narrative is sparse in certain places, while at other times it provides rich detail about Moses' challenges and achievements. To gain further insight about Moses' life, I analyzed traditional commentaries as well as more current works by Aaron Wildavsky, Daniel J. Silver, Emil Bock, and others. The tales in Louis Ginzberg's *Legends of the Jews* revealed the impact Moses has had on Jewish thought. Biblical scholars and fundamentalist interpreters often clash on the meaning and authenticity of the Bible, but the purpose here isn't to engage in that debate. Nor do I wish to hold up Moses as a model of perfect virtue and godliness. Instead, I focus on him as both an inspired leader and a hands-on, very human manager who had to contend with the quintessential uncooperative staff—the "stiff-necked" Israelites.

Moses had to both lead and manage the Children of Israel. Scores of business books have attempted to explain the difference between those two terms, but I found one—Warren Bennis and Burt Nanus's *Leaders*—to be particularly enlightening. According to the authors, "Managers are people who do things right and leaders are people who do the right thing. The difference may be summarized as activities of vision and judgment—*effectiveness*—versus activities of mastering routines—*efficiency*."

People today are often called upon both to lead and manage, as Moses did. The entrepreneur who starts his or her own company must be a visionary who also understands the day-to-day operations of the business. The manager who hires on at a large corporation must share and promote the vision of the CEO or risk losing the confidence of the staff. Part of Moses' genius is that he was able to grow into these roles. While he possessed certain innate characteristics of leadership—such as commitment, tenacity, and a passion for justice—he had to learn many elements of leadership and management on the job. Analyzing how he did it—how he resolved conflicts, created rules and rituals, dealt with his people's complaints and lack of skills, and kept everyone inspired over forty years—provides us with a wealth of practical information.

Moses had no grandiose ideas about his position. He just trusted in God and kept moving forward. The Bible describes him as the humblest of men, and perhaps that is why he was willing to experiment, take advice from others, and act on faith where more experienced leaders might have balked. Time and again

Moses demonstrated leadership traits that are highly prized today. Because we live in the information age, where "facts" evolve daily and the global marketplace is constantly shifting beneath our feet, the skills Moses used to lead his people through the wilderness are extremely relevant: being flexible, thinking quickly, sustaining the confidence of your people in uncertain times, and creating rules that work for individuals from widely diverse backgrounds. When we study why he made the choices he did and understand the reasoning behind his laws, this knowledge can guide us through similar circumstances in our own wilderness.

Bennis and Nanus list and refute five myths of management that I found to be strikingly relevant to the story of Moses. These myths are:

1. Leadership is a rare skill.
2. Leaders are born, not made.
3. Leaders are charismatic.
4. Leadership exists only at the top of an organization.
5. The leader controls, directs, prods, manipulates.

As you read through the 50 Leadership Lessons that follow, you'll see these myths dispelled one by one. Moses not only learned the skills of leadership from

God, he also taught those skills to others. He certainly was not born to the role; contrary to the film versions of his life, the Bible never implies that Moses was inclined to lead anything more than his father-in-law's sheep prior to his encounter with God. There is no biblical evidence that points to his being charismatic either, although he was undoubtedly passionate about his beliefs. And rather than controlling and manipulating people, Moses realized from the beginning that he would have to win the Israelites' trust and cooperation before they would trust in God. Pharaoh controlled and manipulated; Moses inspired and empowered.

The most relevant of Bennis and Nanus's myths is "Leadership exists only at the top of an organization," which implies flying solo. Moses was blessed with an extended management team to assist and advise him throughout his journey, and he recognized the value of cultivating leadership at all levels of his organization. From the earliest days of the Exodus, Moses began to delegate power and responsibility. He appointed magistrates and judges so that the people could learn to govern themselves. His whole enterprise depended on the "children" of Israel growing up and taking on adult responsibilities.

As a rabbi, all too often I hear, "Sure, I'll join the committee, but I don't want to be chairman." Society desperately needs leaders at all levels. We need men and women who are willing not only to do things right, but also to do the right thing. If the story of Moses teaches us anything, it is that you don't have to be perfect to lead brilliantly. Indeed, there is no such thing as a perfect leader. At your company, at the PTA, at your local community center, church, or synagogue, you can step up and become a leader, if only for a season or semester. Without leaders who have vision and a strong moral compass, we'll never progress as a society, no matter how affluent we become.

In this book I've tried to distill the ideas and strategies that are most likely to encourage people to succeed as managers and leaders. It is divided into three parts. Part One deals with issues of communication and motivation. Part Two reveals the tactics Moses used to galvanize his people during the long trek in the Sinai desert. Part Three explores some of the ethical guidelines Moses created. It's my hope that the insights readers gain from these lessons will help them thrive in whatever leadership roles they assume.

—David Baron
Los Angeles, 1999

MOSES:
An Executive Summary

MOSES WAS BORN ROUGHLY THREE THOUSAND YEARS AGO into an Egypt ruled by a bloodthirsty and paranoid pharaoh. Desperate to deplete the Hebrew slave population, which he feared would rise up against him, Pharaoh decreed that every newborn Hebrew boy be put to death. To save her son, Moses' mother placed him in a basket and set him adrift on the Nile, where he was rescued by Pharaoh's daughter and raised as her son in the royal court. When he was grown, Moses ventured off the palace grounds and saw an Egyptian taskmaster beating a Hebrew slave. Moses killed the taskmaster and as a result had to flee Egypt. He sought refuge in Midian, a nearby desert territory.

In Midian Moses began a new life as a shepherd. One day, while tending his flock, he noticed a bush that was aflame but not consumed by the fire. He approached it and God revealed Himself to Moses, charging him with the mission of bringing the Hebrew slaves out of Egypt and delivering them to Canaan— the Promised Land.

Moses' first task was to confront Pharaoh and demand freedom for the Israelites. When Pharaoh refused, God brought ten plagues down upon Egypt. Finally Pharaoh relented and the Israelites departed. The next day, however, the ruler changed his mind and sent his armies to recapture the Israelites, who had just arrived at the Red Sea (Sea of Reeds). Moses urged the group to walk into the waves. As they did, the waters receded and the people crossed to the far shore, with Pharaoh's army in hot pursuit. As the last Israelite reached dry land, the waters closed again, drowning the Egyptians.

Jubilant at their success, the Israelites traveled to Mount Sinai, at the summit of which God presented Moses with the Ten Commandments carved on a pair of stone tablets. When Moses descended to the valley where his people were camped, he saw that they had already broken a commandment—"You shall have no other gods besides me"—and were worshiping a golden calf. Enraged, Moses smashed the tablets and punished those who had disobeyed the Lord. God threatened to destroy the entire community for their transgression, but Moses objected, pleading the case of those Israelites who had not sinned. God relented, a second pair of tablets was carved, and the Children of Israel journeyed on.

Soon thereafter, God and Moses realized that the former slaves would not be hardy enough to conquer

Canaan. The decision was made to wander in the desert for forty years, until a new, stronger generation came of age. In the decades that followed, Moses guided the Hebrew people through their metamorphosis, transforming them into a powerful nation unified by its faith in God. He did this, in large part, by creating 613 commandments that covered nearly every aspect of civilized life, including how to worship, work together, stay healthy, deal with one another justly, and celebrate God's blessings.

After the forty years had passed, Moses and his people gathered at the banks of the Jordan River, which marked the border of Canaan. At last the Israelites were prepared to conquer the territory, with Joshua, Moses' hand-picked successor, as their leader. Moses himself would not be joining them; many years earlier he had disregarded one of God's instructions, and for that offense God refused to let him enter the Promised Land.

Moses died atop Mount Nebo, where he was able to gaze upon the lush country his people would soon inhabit. "No one knows his burial place to this day," says the Bible. "Moses was a hundred and twenty years old when he died; his eyes were undimmed and his vigor unabated....Never again did there arise in Israel a prophet like Moses."

Part One

DELIVERING THE MESSAGE

From the earliest chapters of Exodus we know that Moses was neither an eloquent speaker nor a "natural" leader. After he reluctantly agreed to accept the position of liberator, he faced the daunting task of convincing the enslaved Israelites to follow him out of Egypt. Far from welcoming Moses as a hero, the slaves were skeptical and often downright hostile to him. Moses found that delivering his message would require much more than announcing God's plan and waiting for the troops to rally round.

For Moses to succeed in his mission, he had to exude confidence in his role as messenger and leader. God constantly prodded him forward, and gradually, through doing the job, Moses' confidence grew. He first had to assess the will and commitment of his people and develop strategies for communicating with them. God gave him a brilliant mission statement—the Ten Commandments—but Moses' imagination, compassion, and tenacity also proved invaluable. Moses gradually established a bond with the suspicious Israelites and instilled in them a faith so strong that not even Pharaoh's army could turn them from their goal. He earned his people's trust not once but many times during the course of their journey together. After the initial push out of Egypt, Moses kept God's message alive in the hearts of the Israelites for another forty years, until they reached the Promised Land.

Part One reveals how Moses won the confidence of his people, successfully delivered God's message, and made that message ever more vital with each passing year.

I

Allow Others to Recognize Your Strengths and Recognize the Strengths in Others

"No really great man ever thought himself so" wrote the nineteenth-century English essayist William Hazlitt. Moses, the man who would lead the Israelites out of Egypt and create a new nation, was not a glory seeker. He would have been happy to stay in the desert wilderness of Midian and live out his life raising his family and minding his father-in-law's sheep. When destiny called, he was none too pleased.

"Who am I that I should go to Pharaoh?" was Moses' first reaction to God's offer. "Don't worry," replied the Lord, "I will be with you." Moses tried a different approach: "What if they do not believe me and do not listen to me?" No problem, replied God— He would put enough miracles in Moses' hand that everyone would respect his authority as God's messenger. Next, Moses resorted to his lack of job skills: "Please, O Lord, I have never been a man of words...I am slow of speech and tongue...Make somebody else Your agent!" But God knew He had chosen the right man. "Okay, already," He said. "There is your brother, Aaron...He shall speak for you to the people." Finally, having run out of excuses, Moses accepted the job.

Many of us can relate to Moses' terror of being placed in a high position. We know that the higher our position, the farther we have to fall. Sometimes it's easier to make excuses about our inadequacies than it is to take on the challenge. Even if we don't verbalize our ambivalence to the person offering us the job, we may still be plagued by self-doubt. Like Moses, we may worry that people will laugh when they see us in a position of authority. We may fret that we don't have the right skills for the job. Sometimes, if we're lucky, our boss—or our destiny—will be so implacable that we'll have no choice but to step up to bat and rise to the challenge.

An ancient legend tells us that God actually chose Moses to lead the Hebrew people because of an incident that occurred while he was minding the herd. A kid was separated from the herd and had become lost. Moses ran after it for a long time until he finally found it, exhausted and hungry. He found water for the animal, then hoisted it on his shoulders and returned it to the flock. Seeing this, the Lord thought, "If he shows so much compassion to one lost kid, how much more will he show to the people!" So when Moses claimed he wasn't good enough for the job, God knew otherwise.

We are seldom aware of the criteria higher-ups use when selecting us for positions of leadership. Moses thought speaking skills would be crucial to any great leader, but God disagreed. The attributes God was looking for were strength of character and compassion, and those Moses possessed in abundance. In his management classic *Leaders*, Warren Bennis says that of the leadership qualities most organizations look for, "judgment and character...are the most difficult to identify, measure, or develop. We certainly don't know how to teach them," he says. "Business schools barely try....Although a lot of executives are derailed (or plateaued) for lack of character or judgment, we've never observed a premature career ending for lack of technical competence." Technical competence can be learned or deepened on the job.

As a manager, you are often in a position to encourage people to take on new challenges. When you see potential in others that they do not yet see in themselves, it can be just as difficult to broaden their views as it was to broaden your own. Yet that is part of your job. When God was persuading Moses, He helped Moses make the leap. When Moses said he felt unworthy, God said, "Don't worry, I will be with you." As a manager, you will find it necessary to assure others that although they'll be venturing into new territory, you'll be there for them when they need you. That kind of support is the greatest gift you can give as a manager. When Moses expressed his fear that his authority would not be recognized, God gave him tangible symbols of authority, such as the shepherd's staff that could generate miracles. Similarly, if you put a person into a position of authority, you may have to provide some symbols of that authority—an office with a view, a preferred parking space—so that others in your organization can see that this person really does have new power. Finally, when Moses complained that he lacked a certain skill he thought he needed for the job, God arranged to have Aaron support him in his weak area. You may also have to give the new manager loyal lieutenants.

Like any successful leader, God discerned the traits of leadership in Moses before Moses himself was aware of them. He didn't just give Moses the job assignment and send him on his way. He supported and reassured him, and gave him the tools he needed to succeed. The Sapient Corporation, based in Cambridge, Massachusetts, is an example of a company that has shown remarkable skill at developing leaders. By maintaining its outstanding staff, Sapient has built a reputation for excellence in client service and technological smarts. Jon Frey, a director at Sapient, lists five core values the company looks for when it selects and grooms its leaders: "One of those is client focus: How well does this person make clients happy by understanding and solving their business problems?" Sapient's second core value is leadership, which they measure by how well a person inspires the team and creates a shared vision. They also focus on how well a person motivates people and understands what they need, both personally and professionally, to be happy as people. Finally, they consider openness a core value: How well does the person communicate with others? How approachable and forthright is he or she?

Technical skill is certainly an essential element at Sapient, but in grooming its leaders, the company puts immense emphasis on a person's ability to see potential in others and help them maximize it. Of his stint as a manager on one of Sapient's larger projects, Frey says, "My role was one hundred percent keeping the team happy and supporting them."

God could have brought the Children of Israel out of Egypt any way He wanted to. He could have beamed them up or put them on a magic carpet flying straight to the Promised Land. But He didn't do that. Even with the advantage of His omnipotence, He chose to cultivate leadership talent in Moses and Aaron, and then made sure that they cultivated leadership among the elders of the Israelites.

By seeing the core character traits that lay at the heart of leadership—honesty, integrity, compassion, and courage—and by challenging people to manifest those qualities within themselves, God set in motion more than the Exodus from Egypt. He set in motion a concept of leadership that allowed powerful, universal laws of life to be transmitted to others.

2

Cultivate the Inner Qualities of Leadership

If you had been standing beside Moses at the burn-ing bush, you might have understood exactly why he asked God, "Who am I that I should go to Pharaoh and free the Israelites from Egypt?" We tend to expect a great leader to be charismatic, eloquent, and most of all, eager to lead, and yet Moses was none of these. He stammered, he had lived as an isolated shepherd for twenty years, and he fervently did *not* want the job. Still, God insisted he take it. Why?

By that time in his life Moses was a shepherd, a husband and father, and a man of the wilderness—perhaps he was ready to hear the inner voice calling him. Or perhaps God knew that Moses possessed certain internal qualities that would make him the right leader for the Children of Israel. The Ten Commandments were going to require the Israelites to drastically alter their behavior. If they were to accomplish this mind-bending shift, they would need the inspiration of a leader who could actually live by those rules, not just sermonize about them. Moses fit the bill. His natural compassion and instinct for justice made it easy for him to take the Commandments to heart. He had the maturity to rein in his lusts; he understood the value of self-control; and as a shepherd he had learned to look after his flock. Although Moses was reticent to speak, when he did, his words rang with conviction. And when he acted, he acted with that same conviction.

The importance of actions over ideas—"deeds versus creeds"—is beautifully illustrated in a passage of the Talmud where God and Moses are discussing the Children of Israel. The Lord says, "Better that they should not believe in Me but observe My laws (of human kindness) than believe in Me but not observe My laws." Given God's priorities, it's clear that Moses, for all his external liabilities, had the right stuff for the job. We see this very early on in the Exodus, when the Children of Israel declare their allegiance to God but crumble at the first pangs of hunger. Countless times over the next forty years the Israelites want to return to Egypt, and each time

Moses' own fortitude, along with his steady faith, inspires them to pick themselves up and keep going.

But what of the fact that Moses didn't *want* to lead the Israelites to freedom? Shakespeare says, "Some are born great; some achieve greatness; some have greatness thrust upon them." Many extraordinary leaders have had greatness thrust upon them; reluctance to lead is no indication of whether a person will be good at leading. In fact, an ego-driven desire to "take charge" is sometimes at odds with the inner qualities of great leadership. Daniel Goleman touched on this in an essay entitled "What Makes a Leader?" Goleman observed that the personal styles of great leaders vary: "Some leaders are subdued and analytical." The most effective leaders, in Goleman's opinion, all have a high degree of what he calls *emotional intelligence.*

Goleman breaks down this emotional intelligence into five components: self-awareness, self-regulation, motivation, empathy, and social skill. The actual desire to lead, you'll note, is not among these components. Although Moses may have been lacking in social skills, he had his brother Aaron to assist him, and he was strongly developed in the other four areas.

In recent times, one man has emerged as the epitome of the reluctant but inspiring leader. "I've become president of a club I didn't want to join," Christopher

Reeve told a reporter from the *Wall Street Journal* in 1996. Since Reeve was thrown from a horse in 1995 and left a quadriplegic, he has become an outspoken leader and supremely effective advocate for spinal injury research—so much so that the entire field has been galvanized by his presence.

After he came out of intensive care, Reeve told the same paper, "I began to realize the way it works in this country. We identify with famous people." So he put himself in the public eye and began raising money for the cause. His motivation was simple: He wanted a cure for himself and the other 1.25 million people worldwide who suffer from spinal cord injuries. A cure could only happen if researchers got more funding.

Reeve's efforts led the National Institutes of Health to raise their budget for spinal cord research nineteen percent, to $56 million, and set off a wave of private donations. Because of Reeve, spinal cord research is now a more vital field. Wise Young, of Rutgers University's Spinal Cord Injury Project, reported in the *Wall Street Journal*, "We used to have one [research] breakthrough a year. The last two years, we've had one a month." It shows what impact a single leader can have on a seemingly impossible goal.

Other well-known people have suffered paralyzing injuries—General George Patton and jockey Willie

Shoemaker, to name just two—but Reeve has a unique public persona. Seeing the man who played Superman in a wheelchair brings home the reality that it can happen to any of us. Reeve is often quoted as saying that he has only one wish: to be able to hug his children. The remark tends to make people aware of the gifts they already possess and spurs them to use those gifts. If you can hug your child, he seems to be saying, lend me a hand so that I can one day hug mine.

Moses faced a similar challenge. Yes, you're hungry, he told the Israelites. You're hot, thirsty, suffering, and in pain. But you have freedom! Recognize your gifts and use them. Moses was able to get that message across not because he was such a skillful orator but because he was persistent, motivated, and dedicated to his cause. Reeve takes the same long-term approach with respect to his mission to find a cure for spinal cord paralysis. "I'm pretty tenacious," he told the *Wall Street Journal*.

The qualities of faith, compassion, drive, self-control, and persistence are the attributes that make a great leader. Forget the stereotype of the charismatic firebrand pep-talking his team into a frenzy. Instead, cultivate the inner qualities of leadership.

3

Speak to People on Their Own Level, and Make It Personal

GOD CHOSE MOSES TO BE THE ONE MAN TO WHOM HE would "speak mouth to mouth, plainly and not in riddles." The only time He addressed the Israelites directly was at Mount Sinai, where amid a terrifying natural display, He delivered the Ten Commandments.

"All the people witnessed the thunder and lightning, the blare of the horn and the mountain smoking; and when the people saw it, they fell back and stood at a distance. 'You speak to us,' they said to Moses, 'and we will obey; but let not God speak to us, lest we die.'" The Israelites wanted direct, human communication. Moses complied.

"Moses went down to the people and spoke to them," relates the Bible in a sentence that sums up the thrust of Moses' life. To transmit God's law, he walked among the people and demonstrated that law to them. He could have set himself apart; he could have delivered a speech from the heights of Mount Sinai. But if the Israelites were going to listen and accept the message, Moses had to deliver it in their language, on their level.

It's a well-worn business maxim that a leader should walk among the people, but there's a big difference between going through the motions and being sincere about them. There's an art to speaking to people on their level without being condescending. As a rabbi, one of the first challenges I faced was finding common ground with people whose paths I might never have crossed in everyday life. After twenty-five years, I've learned some fundamental rules that are important in both the business world and the social realm.

To begin, it's crucial that people sense who you are when you talk to them. The quickest way to achieve this is to go where they are, be it a building site, a production line, a sales office, or a school yard. Talking to people on their own turf makes you more accessible than if you were seated behind your desk or, in my case, standing behind a lectern on a raised platform above the congregation. I make a practice of always memorizing my sermons as opposed to reading them, so I can leave the lectern and walk among the seated congregants. That way, in addition to giving the sermon, I can ask questions and make sure everyone is participating in the conversation. All of this makes me more human and accessible and intensifies the congregation's relationship with me. They hear my message not as some lofty pronouncement but as a tangible goal.

There is an old tradition, dating from the days of Ezra the Scribe, of bringing the Bible to the marketplace for public reading on Mondays and Thursdays. There, amid the din of commerce, people would hear God's words on the busiest shopping days of the week. The ancients knew well the value of making your message accessible.

Leadership ability depends on more than the way you speak to large groups, however. The real test is how you speak to people one-on-one. Bobby Spivak is the founder of a nationwide chain of restaurants called The Daily Grill. He is a master at "people skills," although I doubt he's ever given much thought to his technique. He's just a naturally warm person who really does care about his employees and remember details about their lives. Recently I met Bobby for lunch at one of his Los Angeles locations. As we were walking in, one of his employees—a dishwasher—was on his way out. Bobby called him by his first name, stopped him, asked how his family was, and chatted a bit about goings-on in the city.

I'm always impressed at the ease with which Bobby can talk to anyone, and I know the dividends it pays. He's trying to establish a successful chain of restaurants, and the chain is only as good as each individual Grill. As founder and CEO, Bobby is acutely aware of the link between employee loyalty and quality work.

Chatting intelligently with everyone from the dishwasher to the mayor comes naturally to Bobby Spivak, but most of us have to be a little more deliberate about it. To make your conversations with people more personal, you should always try to do two things: Be specific and focus on the other person's needs.

The more specific you are when talking to another person, the more sincere you'll sound. In fact, being specific forces you to *be* sincere, not just sound as if you are. "How's the family?" doesn't come across nearly as genuine as "How's the kids' new school? Is Lucy still on the basketball team?" Attaching real names to the family conjures up their images and makes you think about them.

Obviously, the more people with whom you come into contact, the harder it is to keep accurate mental files of all this personal data. But you can convey the same level of sincerity by being specific about the information *you're* delivering. Stephanie Sherman, author of *Make Yourself Memorable,* offers an excellent illustration of this. Instead of uttering well-meaning but shallow phrases such as "I really appreciate that," be specific about what you appreciate and why. For example, "I appreciate your taking the time to help me with this software because you've saved me hours of frustration trying to figure it out on my own." Specificity makes it personal, and personal contact intensifies your relationship with others. The more intense that relationship is, the more committed they will be to you and your mission.

Over the years I've had congregants from all walks of life, multimillionaires and day laborers, Ph.D.s and folks who never completed high school. Because much of my job involves counseling people in private, I've had to find ways to communicate with all of them, regardless of their background. I learned long ago that surface differences fall away when I focus on what the other person needs.

Years ago, when I headed a congregation in Miami, Florida, I received a call from a wealthy congregant whose mother had just died. He wanted to consult with me about funeral arrangements right away, but I was visiting my family in New York City. The man flew me on his private jet to his estate in Palm Beach. The surroundings were breathtaking: great works of art, magnificent furnishings, parklike grounds. We sat in a lavish room watching the ocean glitter outside the windows.

"Typically a family member delivers the eulogy," I began. "Do you want to do that, or would you like me to?"

As the conversation unfolded, it became clear that although he wanted to do something significant for his mother, they hadn't been close. In fact, the relationship had been a very painful one for this gentleman. As I listened carefully and watched his anguished expression, the externals became irrelevant. It didn't matter that the room we sat in was fit for a czar; the core issue was his conflict over his relationship with his mother.

My role as a rabbi—and the role of any manager or friend, for that matter—is to listen for the core issue. If you're a good listener, you'll recognize that we're all human and the issues are all going to be pretty much the same. You can let the other person blow off steam, or strut and display bravado, or use whatever crutch he or she may need, but if you listen carefully you'll hear the core issue. It will be familiar to you, no matter what their walk of life.

In the case of this congregant, I suggested that we find a way to remember his mother in a dignified fashion and use the funeral service to begin burying the hostility he felt toward her. Our sanctuary needed a new eternal light to suspend over the holy ark. I felt that this would be a fitting tribute, one that would cause him to remember his mother in a positive light, both figuratively and literally, each time he entered the sanctuary. He agreed that this would work; it would allow him to demonstrate his respect without having to deliver an emotional public eulogy. By listening carefully, I was able to provide what he needed to resolve his core issue.

Speaking to people on their level, then, means more than simply walking among them. It means intensifying your personal relationship with them by being specific when you talk and listening for their core issues.

The day before Moses died, the Lord insisted that he deliver a poem to the Israelites warning them of His wrath should they stray from the covenant. Moses recited the stern and formal verses as ordered. Then, exhausted and only hours from death, he added, "Take to heart all the words with which I have warned you this day…For this is not a trifling thing for you: it is your very life." Until the end, Moses not only delivered the message but made it personal.

4
Ask for What You Want

God didn't sugarcoat the situation when he laid out His plan for Moses at the burning bush. "Ask Pharaoh for freedom," He instructed, "yet I know the king of Egypt will let you go only because of a greater might." If Pharaoh was going to rebuff Moses, what was the purpose of asking him for freedom in the first place?

Moses knew Pharaoh wouldn't grant his request to free the slaves, but he came asking for a smaller concession—three days in the wilderness for the Hebrews to worship. If Pharaoh had shown some flexibility there, Moses might have chosen a different strategy for the rest of the struggle. But there was no flexibility; in fact, Pharaoh responded by heaping more burdens upon the slaves. Moses now knew where he stood and announced the first plague.

Taking the direct approach—going to the person who has something you want and asking for it—is an invaluable strategy not just in business but also in every realm of life. Yet people shy away from it, usually because they're intimidated. Oftentimes they don't want to overstep their bounds, or mix business with pleasure, or be perceived as too aggressive. Most of all, they don't want to be rejected. Because so many people are reluctant to ask for what they want, if you do so, you'll gain a huge advantage.

One way to test this theory is to talk to a successful real estate agent. Good agents are always on the lookout for desirable properties, and they don't hesitate to ask the owners of such properties if they would consider selling. Most of the time the answer is no, but every now and then an owner replies, "Well, for the right price..." By asking directly, the agent might get to represent a property that's worth a good part of a year's income.

You never know until you ask. One day, as I sat in the stands at my son's ice hockey game, I struck up a conversation with the father of another boy. I had never thought to ask him what he did for a living, and it turned out he was the president of a graphics company. As we watched the kids play hockey, I told him about a problem I was having with my prototype for a company called Image Movement Technology. We were developing electronic signs that displayed a roll of twenty images and switched from image to image in under a second. The problem was, we couldn't find a suitable material on which to print the images. Paper was too fragile and kept disintegrating at high speeds; film was too rigid.

"Let me send you some stuff I just got from Asia," he offered. A few days later I received a sample of a synthetic paper that looks like the finest matte stock but is incredibly durable—you can't rip it. The print quality is better than that of paper, and it's opaque enough to be backlit. We redesigned our prototype to incorporate the synthetic paper, and our long-standing problem was finally solved.

Was I overstepping my bounds by confiding my business dilemma to this man? At worst, he could have given me the cold shoulder and we both would have returned to watching the game. As it was, this chance interaction saved me months more work and research expenses.

Even if you are certain your request will be denied, ask. There's always the possibility that you're wrong—that the other person will say yes. Equally important, if you do get rebuffed, the rejection itself will provide you with vital information about the other party's position.

Edgar Bronfman Sr. learned the value of asking for what he wanted at the outset of his famous campaign to restore to Holocaust victims their assets in Swiss banks. Bronfman, sixty-nine, is the chairman of the multi-billion-dollar Seagram empire. He's been involved with the World Jewish Congress since the early 1980s, when Israel Singer and Elan Steinberg approached him to join and help rejuvenate the organization. In the mid-1990s, they asked for his advice on how to retrieve the gold and other assets stolen by Nazis and quietly deposited in so-called heirless Swiss bank accounts.

"I don't know why nobody looked at this question for 50 years," Bronfman told *Maclean's* magazine in June 1997. "Europeans, I think, have a sense, 'leave well enough alone.'" Bronfman had the idea of asking for reparation for Holocaust survivors and their descendants. In September 1995 he traveled to Bern, Switzerland, to meet with officials of the Swiss Banks Association regarding the lost assets. In Bronfman's words: "We were ushered into a small room with no furniture and left standing. That was enough to irritate me. I don't treat people that way and I don't expect to be treated that way. We waited about eight to ten minutes and then they stormed into the room." The bankers told Bronfman they had found 775 dormant bank accounts worth $32 million, and that they'd be willing to hand over that amount. "It occurred to me—thinking very quickly, actually on no sleep—that if they are offering $32 million, there's got to be an awful lot more. Why would they offer anything at all, if there really wasn't anything there?"

Listening is an important part of asking—just sitting back and listening and observing what the response is. Bronfman left Bern empty-handed, but his meeting was a success. It told him that the Swiss did indeed have Jewish assets; in fact, they probably had lots more than they were admitting. Bronfman and the WJC demanded an investigation of the Swiss role in handling gold and goods plundered by the Nazis. The eyes of the world focused for the first time on reputedly neutral Switzerland. After a year and a half of negative publicity, the pressure worked. In March 1997, the Swiss government made another offer: Instead of $32 million, it offered a $6.2 *billion* fund for victims of Nazis and a separate $270 million fund, backed by Swiss banks and industry, solely for Holocaust survivors.

Whether your request is met with great enthusiasm, lukewarm interest, or outright hostility, you will always be in a better position for having asked. You'll either gain what you want or obtain information about how to get it. If all you find out is the level of difficulty you'll be facing—as Moses learned with Pharaoh—you'll still be better informed than you were before. "Ask, and it will be given you," said Jesus, another great leader. "Seek, and you will find; knock, and it will be opened to you."

5
Let Them Know Your Ways

By the time Moses arrived with the Israelites at Mount Sinai, he had a pretty good idea of how capricious the Lord could be. God described Himself as "jealous," and the Bible is full of instances where His behavior is unpredictable, to say the least.

At the summit of Mount Sinai, Moses' frustration with God finally bursts forth. He has already made the climb once, rushed down to deal with the insurrection at the golden calf, punished the faithless, and trudged back up the mountain. Now his nerves are wearing thin, and he confronts God: "See, You say to me, 'Lead this people forward,' but You have not made known to me whom You will send with me. Further, You have said, 'I have singled you out by name, and you have, indeed, gained my favor.' Now, if I have truly gained

Your favor, pray let me know Your ways, that I may know You and continue in Your favor."

This scene illustrates a major lesson for managers at all levels: If you want people to follow your plan, they have to know it. This seems obvious, but many policies and change initiatives fail because management doesn't bother to communicate the changes to everyone in the organization. Especially when "the plan" varies from quarter to quarter, it is vital to make sure everyone affected is aware of the changes.

You might be in a pivotal position to make sure policies are translated from the realm of ideas to the realm of action. Just as Moses made certain he had God's message straight before relaying it to the Israelites, you need to check with your superiors regularly about the current plan, and then tell your staff what that plan is and how they fit into it.

When people lose touch with the message, they lose their sense of connection with the company. On a more basic level, they can't perform their best if they don't know what they're supposed to be doing. Elizabeth Danziger, president of Worktalk Communication Consulting, recently told me about an incident that highlights the dangers of not communicating the plan. "A food-processing company faced a crisis," she said. "They had lost several million dollars in revenues over the past few years, and they felt that their relationships with their sales representatives had deteriorated significantly. They asked us to help them improve their communication with the reps. The owner showed me a graph of their sales revenues for the past ten years. At a point about three years earlier, the revenues had dropped precipitously and had not risen since. 'What happened that year?' I asked.

" 'Oh, that was the year we changed our marketing focus and decided to support a different product area,' they replied.

" 'Did you inform your sales reps of the change?' I asked.

" 'No,' they admitted. They had diminished their support for the items their sales representatives were accustomed to selling and had developed new, potentially more profitable products—with marketing support now focused on those. The reason for the lost revenue seemed clear: They hadn't informed their sales reps of the changes. Consequently, the reps were selling fewer of the traditional products, yet not realizing they should push the new products."

When change is happening rapidly, it's even more crucial to keep everyone informed. Unfortunately, the pressure to plunge ahead *without* communicating often becomes intense as well. In September 1998, *USA*

Today reported that "communication mishaps are eroding productivity and leaving employers at a competitive
disadvantage, new studies show. The blunders can
crush morale, especially during times of widespread
change."

Dr. Nathaniel Branden, in his book *Self-Esteem at
Work,* states that "to encourage the practice of operating consciously a manager must provide easy access not
only to the information people need to do their work
but also about the wider context in which they work—
the goals and progress of the organization, market
conditions in general, the activities of the competitors—so that they are always operating with the clear-
est grasp of context possible."

As a manager, your gains will be enormous if you
regularly confirm the organization's plan with your
superiors and explain it to your team in a way they all
can understand. "Otherwise, people live with fear,
doubt, and confusion," says Peter Giuliano, chairman
of Executive Communications Group in Englewood,
New Jersey. "If you allow that to happen as a corporate leader, shame on you."

Moses beseeched the Lord to "let me know Your
ways, that I may know You and continue in Your
favor." On a spiritual level he may have been seeking
knowledge of God, but on a practical level he was con-

cerned about getting the message straight because he understood that if he relayed the wrong message, he would fall out of favor. For your sake as well as that of your staff, take the time to clarify the message and let your team know your ways.

6

Use a Mission Statement as Your Ten Commandments

The Bible recounts that "Moses went and repeated to the people all the commands of the Lord and all the rules. And the people answered with one voice, saying, 'All the things the Lord has commanded us we will do.' Moses then wrote down all the commands of the Lord.

"Early in the morning Moses set up an altar at the foot of the mountain, with twelve pillars for the twelve tribes of Israel ... [The Children of Israel] offered burnt offerings ... Then he took the record of the covenant and read it aloud to the people. And they said, 'All the Lord has spoken we will faithfully do.'"

If Moses was to be effective in communicating God's mission, he knew he'd have to approach the people from all angles. He couldn't just announce, "Here's the mission statement" and retreat to his tent. When Moses set up the altar with twelve pillars, he was in essence saying, "You are all a part of this." He was giving the Israelites a concrete symbol of their connection to the Lord and his laws. The Lord's covenant (the Ten Commandments) would be housed within the shelter of those twelve pillars, and the people would protect and preserve God's word.

After the altar was in place, Moses again removed the covenant and read it aloud to the people. This time they were so involved that they volunteered not just to do as the Lord commanded but to do it *"faithfully."* Reading the commands aloud, writing them down, establishing a special place for them, reciting them again—this is how Moses reinforced his message and infused the Israelites with the ideals of Judaism.

Prior to Moses, the history of the Israelites had been an entirely oral one. Traditionalists believe Moses himself wrote the first five books of the Bible, but even if you take the more scholarly view that various authors worked on it, one fact remains absolute: The Ten Commandments were the first written laws of the people. The subsequent ritual "commands" were somewhat complex, but the Ten Commandments, or "utterances," as they were called, were simple and to the point. Some scholars even believe they were originally one-word edicts—"No-kill," "No-steal"—that biblical authors embellished centuries after the fact. In Moses' day, the Ten Commandments were easy to repeat, easy to remember, and powerfully clear. They had to be, if they were going to impress the throng gathered at the foot of Mount Sinai.

We tend to think of the escaped slaves as a cohesive band of Jewish families, but the Bible tells us it was a "mixed multitude" that fled Egypt with Moses. Along with the Israelites, the multitude included western Semitic tribes, Nubians, and others. Furthermore, the Israelites themselves were a loose-knit confederation of tribes whose bonds had been worn thin by the brutality of slave life. To pull this diverse group together, Moses needed a mission statement that could be recalled, translated, sung, or written down by every person in the crowd. The Ten Commandments served that purpose brilliantly.

Today's leaders could also benefit from a brief set of guiding principles that are easy to remember and reinforce—and some have realized it. A friend of mine worked at Sarnoff Corporation, whose mission is the "creation and commercialization of innovative electronic, biomedical, and information technologies that change our world." That statement along with a compact expression of the company's business vision, strategy, and values, are printed on a wallet-size card that is handed to each new employee when he or she first arrives. The employees are asked to keep the card in their wallets and look at it often.

It's truly impressive that Sarnoff, a highly complex enterprise, has managed to get its mission, vision, strategy, and values onto a single wallet-size card. Someone at the top clearly understands the value of establishing simple guidelines and writing them down. In addition to the mission statement, the items on the little card include:

Business vision
+ Tenfold growth in ten years

Strategy
+ client first
+ extraordinary staff
+ creative solutions to client needs
+ be the best; partner with the best
+ deliver on time, on budget
+ global presence
+ employee rewards for client success

Values
+ absolute integrity
+ champions

- respect for the individual
- productive teamwork
- tenacity and creativity
- power of diversity
- listening to understand
- compelling communications
- community involvement
- hard work; having fun; making a difference

It's equally impressive that employees carry these cards in their wallets. Although many companies post guidelines like these on bulletin boards, to have employees actually carrying them in their wallets is akin to Moses installing the covenant within the twelve pillars. In your wallet, the card automatically becomes one of your personal belongings.

The card is not just impressive as a concept, it is also effective in real life, as I learned from a former Wall Street banker who joined Sarnoff to identify potentially marketable new technologies. This was no ten-year-old memorizing the Girl Scout law—was the card too simple to motivate people like her?

"Not at all," she asserted when I posed this question. "I was extremely excited about working at Sarnoff. When I got my business cards, the vision card was at the top of the stack. My manager told me, 'Every time you hand out a business card, glance at this card too.' Sarnoff's goal—to increase business tenfold in ten years—was very ambitious. The only way we were going to achieve it was to concentrate all our efforts on that goal. So I did as he asked; I glanced at the card each time I handed out a business card. It did help me stay focused on Sarnoff's vision, especially when I first joined the company."

People who appear to be "born winners" are often acutely aware of the power that lies in consistently reinforcing the mission. Chamique Holdsclaw, a top player in women's college basketball, has been known to write her goals on her shoes, socks, and sweatbands. In her first national championship game, she strode onto the courts with DEFENSE WINS CHAMPIONSHIPS inked on her sneaker.

As a manager, you can keep your staff fired up about their mission by keeping that mission in front of them and by reminding them how they enhance the company and the community with their work. Reinforce the mission not just at semiannual meetings but every day, and your people are more likely to make the leap from "Okay, I'll do it" to "I'll do it faithfully."

7

Realize That Faith
Must Be Renewed

ONE OF THE REASONS MOSES WAS SO RELUCTANT TO
lead the Israelites was that he seriously doubted they
would follow him: "What if they do not believe me
and do not listen to me?" he asked. They will, the Lord
assured him—with all the signs and powers He would
bestow on Moses, the people would certainly believe.
At first everything went according to plan. Aaron and
Moses gathered the elders of Israel together. Then
"Aaron repeated all the words that the Lord had spoken to Moses, and he performed the signs in the sight
of the people, and the people were convinced."

Not for long. As Moses had feared, the Israelites
turned out to be a hard sell. While many (but by no

means all) of them were glad enough to leave Egypt, they turned on him just days later at the Red Sea (the Sea of Reeds). After God parted the waters, they joyfully accompanied Moses into the desert, but soon their loyalty withered again. They were thirsty, so Moses turned bitter water sweet; they were hungry, so he appealed to God to provide manna and quail. Yet despite these miracles, in the weeks that followed, the Children of Israel still accused Moses of plotting to "kill us and our children and livestock with thirst."

"Before long they'll be stoning me!" Moses cried to the Lord. It seemed to Moses that there was no miracle magnificent enough to convince the Israelites that he knew what he was doing. At every turn, he had to prove himself again.

If parting the Red Sea and drowning Pharaoh's army couldn't earn Moses the confidence of the Israelites as God's messenger, it's not surprising that the average manager has trouble sustaining the confidence of his staff. Most men and women are doubters; they're reluctant to follow anyone into uncertain waters, even a Moses. There is no such thing as winning the people's trust once and for all. Faith must be renewed, no matter how brilliant your past successes. In cynical Hollywood the saying goes, "You're only as good as your last movie."

This aspect of human nature was brought home to me when I interviewed Dr. Jonas Salk in 1995. Salk, who developed the polio vaccine in 1953, was in a reflective mood in what turned out to be the last televised interview he gave before his death.

During our talk I said, "I know you were ridiculed for your research on polio."

"By the entire scientific community," he confirmed. "No one believed it would work. No one thought you could stimulate antibodies by injecting a person with dead virus."

At the time we spoke, Dr. Salk was again involved in pioneering research. Although he was a luminary in the field of public health, winner of a Congressional Gold Medal (among many other awards), and head of the Salk Institute, he was nevertheless experiencing tremendous resistance to his current project. The disease he was researching was AIDS, and his attempts to develop a vaccine for it were being met with the same derision he had encountered forty years earlier. This time, the scientific community insisted that an AIDS vaccine was unfeasible because the virus was able to mutate so quickly.

"I know this will work and I'm doing it," Salk told me. His purity of mission and belief in his approach made all the naysayers irrelevant.

Jonas Salk continued to do his research until his death in June of that year. Just eight months later the *Philadelphia Inquirer* announced, "The final act in the life of Jonas Salk opens today, as large-scale human testing of his experimental AIDS medicine begins." In 1997, the first reports on the vaccine, Remune, were in: the immune cells of people who had taken the drug significantly increased to fight off the HIV virus. Clinical trials of Remune continue as of this writing; on the Web it is referred to simply as the Salk vaccine.

Whenever you present your staff with a new or difficult challenge, the majority of them will dig their heels into the sand and say, "It's impossible. We can't do it. Why have you brought us here?" The only way to gain their faith is to proceed with your mission, unfazed, until your Red Sea finally parts. When that happens—when your impossible idea proves to be viable after all—the crowds will follow you, but be ready when they stop at the next ridge and demand yet another miracle.

Your staff's faith must constantly be rekindled by your vision and energy. "I know how defiant and stiff-necked you are," Moses (never one to mince words) told his people. Be prepared to prove yourself not once, but every time, and you'll win the confidence of your staff the only way it can be won: day by day.

8
Negotiate Face-to-Face

WHEN MOSES DIED, HE WAS BURIED IN AN UNMARKED grave, and "no one knows his burial place to this day," says the Bible. But the final lines of Deuteronomy do provide an epitaph of sorts, which begins: "Never again did there arise in Israel a prophet like Moses— whom the Lord singled out, face to face."

Moses' face-to-face contact with God was the defining element of his life. "The Lord would speak to Moses face to face, as one man speaks to another," the Bible reports. And the Almighty didn't hesitate to remind errant Israelites that "Moses is trusted throughout My household...he beholds the likeness of the Lord." Trust, then, is synonymous with face-to-face contact. In this, Moses and God set an example for human communication.

In every aspect of life, face-to-face is the optimum mode of communication. These days there are countless devices that allow us to avoid looking one another in the eye—telephones, E-mail, faxes, answering machines. There are also institutionalized roadblocks to face-to-face discussions: lawyers, consultants, agents, and so forth. All of these only underscore the value of talking in person. A handshake, delivered with a steady gaze, is still the most valuable tool in any negotiation.

I've personally known the exhilaration of face-to-face negotiations and the disappointment when that personal contact is disrupted. In 1996, I happened to be staying at the same hotel as Fred Rosen, then the CEO of TicketMaster. My own company, Image Movement Technology, was just getting off the ground, and I mentioned it to Fred. He was intrigued and asked if we could meet a few weeks later, which we did. Fred has a quick mind, and he immediately saw how our company—which manufactures mobile moving signs—could integrate with TicketMaster. In ten minutes we had outlined how our alliance would work, including an option for TicketMaster to buy out IMT in five years if the union was successful.

Then it went to the lawyers. Many legal maneuverings later, the negotiations fell apart. Meanwhile, Rosen's attention was diverted, the delays multiplied, and our face-to-face contact was disrupted. As it turned out, TicketMaster was in the process of being acquired by the Home Shopping Network, which pre-occupied Rosen. In the long run it was good luck for us that we weren't tied to TicketMaster—IMT would have been a very small fish in the Home Shopping Network pond. But I often recall the arduous dealings with our respective legal teams in contrast to our original ten-minute negotiation.

If you don't have face-to-face contact, it's hard to reach a conclusion once lawyers, auditors, analysts, and accountants are injected into the process. They are being paid to find potential problems a hundred years down the road, while you want to close the deal and move forward. To sustain the momentum, you must keep meeting face-to-face with the other person, not his or her representatives.

Another incident, which involved a face-to-face meeting that resulted in a quickly consummated agreement, occurred in 1993, when I first met with Stan Seiden, president of the Nederlander Organization. I had spoken with him on the phone on numerous occasions, but when we met in person to discuss whether my temple could lease the landmark Wilshire Theater in Beverly Hills, the meeting took an interesting turn. "I remember that great lecture you gave at my temple five years ago," Stan said. "I was very impressed with your style and message." Over the next forty minutes we shmoozed, swapped jokes, and concluded the agreement. A telephone exchange is never a substitute for the face-to-face encounter.

Across the country, as legal fees skyrocket, face-to-face mediation is being adopted by all types of organizations. The U.S. Postal Service has launched REDRESS (Resolve Employee Disputes Reach Equitable Solutions Swiftly), a program designed to improve workplace relationships and diffuse disputes, especially those involving discrimination. REDRESS gives postal employees who allege discrimination the chance to sit down along with a mediator and resolve their conflicts within fourteen days of a request. Other avenues of dispute resolution often take months and don't involve a face-to-face meeting. In the worst cases, costly lawsuits are filed and workplace tension ratchets up.

An even more startling example of the power of face-to-face communication is the success of programs that mediate between a victim and offender, where a criminal and his victim sit together and explain to each other their experiences of the crime. The misdeeds are usually minor property offenses, and the criminals are most often juveniles. But to the victims, those "minor" crimes can have a serious psychological impact—and when the young offenders meet their victims face-to-face, it can radically alter their perception of their actions.

"It's not uncommon for offenders to perceive themselves as victims, as screwed-over by the system itself," observes Bruce Kittle, director of the University of Wisconsin—Madison Law School's Restorative Justice Project. His cohort, Walter Dickey, agrees: "There is a reason why people commit crimes again and again. A big part of that is lack of empathy on the part of the offender for victims." Interviewed for *The Progressive* (September 1998), Kittle and Dickey expressed great enthusiasm for victim-and-offender mediation. "It may not change everything about the current system," says Dickey, "but the truth of it will win out."

When victim and offender sit down together, remarkable breakthroughs can happen, even in the most serious of crimes. One especially poignant case, reported in the August 1998 issue of *Texas Monthly* magazine, involved a father who waited twelve years to confront his daughter's killer. "I wanted to find the man who did this to my girl, look him in the eye, and say, 'Why the hell did you do this?'" recalled Robert Kimbrew. "It took every ounce of energy and courage I had, but meeting Faryion Wardrop is what kept me sane. After all those years I was finally able to tell him about the horror he had brought into my life. And I saw the sincerity in his face when he said, 'Robert, I am truly sorry.' "

Only in face-to-face discussions can this level of healing begin to take place. No matter how technologically advanced we become, there will never be a substitute for human contact. Take advantage of this fact whenever you want an encounter to carry special weight. Deliver the news, make the deal, and sustain the relationship face-to-face.

9
Maximize Your Second-in-Command

IF YOU EVER NEED PROOF OF THE NECESSITY OF A STRONG second-in-command, consider the relationship between Moses and Aaron. Although Moses was indisputably in charge, his mission would have been impossible without his brother. The obvious reason for this was that Moses had a speech impediment: "I am slow of speech and tongue," is how he put it to the Lord. Aaron, in contrast, was eloquent. Explained God to Moses, "You shall speak to him [Aaron] and put the words in his mouth...and he shall speak for you to the people." It seems a practical solution to a straightforward problem, but as the story of Exodus unfolds, we can further appreciate the ingenuity of this plan.

The most significant effect of Aaron's role as spokesman was that it allowed Moses to maintain a distance from Pharaoh—and from his own people—when he deemed it necessary. Aaron could deliver the news, and Moses could stand back and gauge the reaction. Aaron announced the Lord's plans; Aaron wielded Moses' staff and brought forth the first plagues. But when it came to responding to Pharaoh's anger and speaking *for* God, Moses stepped in. He spoke when his absolute authority was required to further the cause.

Having your second-in-command deliver news that might be met with doubt or anger is a time-tested, invaluable technique. When my son Jonathan was a baby and we'd take him for his periodic checkups and vaccinations, it was the doctor who came in and tickled the baby, gently examined him, and spoke soothingly. Who gave the shots? The nurse. As a result, Jonathan never associated his doctor with pain.

The good guy/bad guy structure isn't subtle, but it works. When director Marshall Herskovitz was making the film *Dangerous Beauty*, he hired a famous Italian costume designer. The actresses in the film were to portray courtesans, and the designer, an extremely talented (and exacting) woman, created dresses true to the period: simple red gowns with little decoration or décolletage.

The instant Herskovitz saw the designs, he knew that they didn't convey the sensuality that was crucial to the characters. He also realized that the designer would object to changing them, and that this could cause delays on their already tight schedule. Herskovitz sent his producer to deliver the bad news. The costume designer threw a fit with the producer, but by the time she sat down with Herskovitz, she had resigned herself to the changes. The schedule was maintained and the film was completed to everyone's satisfaction.

Even if your message isn't shocking or frightening, it may be misunderstood. Your second-in-command can be your buffer. If there is an honest misunderstanding, your employees will still have a higher authority—you—to whom they can complain. If the message is met with howls of protest, you can calculate your next move, then either personally reassert the plan or change it. You can also use your second-in-command to intentionally test an idea on your employees before fully committing yourself to it.

Another key role of the second-in-command is that of mediator. While Moses stood at the top of the leadership ladder transmitting God's laws, Aaron played the part of peacemaker. Here again, he acted as a buffer between Moses and the people. The leader should be seen as an independent voice of reason. You have a good chance of fulfilling that role if you can stay above the fray long enough to weigh the merits of the argument and find out exactly what each side wants.

All this may sound like a bad deal for the second-in-command, but it's only one aspect of the job. Your second is also the person who, next to you, has the most power and responsibility in your organization. Dennis Holt, chairman and chief executive of Western International Media, hired Michael Kassan as his second-in-command after running his company as a one-man show for many years. Holt had once described the situation at Western as "a Zorba the Greek syndrome, with everyone sitting around the bed waiting for him to die." Kassan took on many of Holt's day-to-day duties, while Holt devoted more time to expanding in the United States and overseas.

When I interviewed the two of them, it was clear they were on the same wavelength and that Kassan thoroughly enjoyed the job. They frequently finished each other's sentences—"We know exactly where we need to get without speaking," said Kassan—and although they work long hours, Kassan didn't complain. "Initially, if I didn't know the answer to something, Dennis would be taken aback—'How could you *not* know?' But we learned each other's styles," he said.

It's not surprising that many seconds eventually want to be first. After years of learning the ropes, they are ready to assume control of their own territory. When this happened with Aaron, Moses responded with characteristic foresight. The pressure actually came from the outside—from people accusing Moses of nepotism. Moses' solution was to make Aaron's realm of power distinct from his own. He created the priesthood, with all the rituals and sacrifices that went along with it, and put Aaron at its head. Up until then, Moses and Aaron seemed to be one, their leadership tightly intertwined. Now Aaron had his own turf. Both brothers still worked toward the same goals—reach the Promised Land and worship one God—but Aaron would stand separate from Moses.

It takes a confident leader to invest his second-in-command with this much power. But the move provided Moses with exactly what he needed: It put an end to the complaints about nepotism and kept the Israelites focused and unified. Bear in mind that Aaron didn't carve out his own territory; Moses, at God's command, created it for him. By so doing, Moses could fashion a division—the priesthood—that furthered the goals of the organization.

Anticipate a day when your second-in-command will ask for his or her own territory. It's possible that day will never come, but if the person is talented and ambitious, it probably will. Long before the crisis arrives, give some thought to the sort of "priesthood" that would best serve your goals. By offering the territory rather than waiting to be asked, you have a greater chance of maintaining both the person's loyalty and your control of the big picture.

10

Bring Your Staff Out of the Slave Mentality

M OSES KNEW IT WOULD TAKE ALL HIS POWERS OF PER- suasion to convince the Israelites to leave Egypt with him. He tried to jump-start the process by relaying a pledge from the Almighty: "I will take you to be my people and I will be your God.... I will bring you into the land which I swore to give to Abraham, Isaac, and Jacob, and I will give it to you for a possession, I am the Lord."

What better guarantee could Moses offer? Here was God himself, promising to deliver the people to Canaan if they'd just follow him. It didn't work. "When Moses told this to the Israelites, they would not listen to Moses, their spirits crushed by cruel bondage."

The Israelites had been slaves for generations—as far back as any of them could remember. In an extremely hierarchical society, they had been at the bottom of the heap. Yes, the Lord had vowed to free them, but his promise fell on deaf ears because the Israelites couldn't conceive of being free. It was too far beyond their realm of experience. Years after they had left Egypt, most of them still felt and behaved like slaves. "Their spirits crushed" implies much more than weariness or depression. It means that their perception of themselves had been flattened. This is the essence of the slave mentality: having a limited view of yourself and feeling powerless to control your surroundings. Moses' great challenge was to teach these people how to be free and to show them what self-determination was all about.

Like so many people who have a limited perception of themselves, the Israelites didn't realize exactly what their problem was. No one said to Moses, "But we're just a group of ex-slaves—we don't have the experience or confidence to take care of ourselves." Instead, whenever they were up against a new obstacle, they panicked, pined for Egypt, or murmured against Moses for expecting too much of them. Every experience that could have been a growth opportunity, from escaping Pharaoh's army, to finding quail and manna, to receiving the Ten Commandments, was lost on most of them because they viewed themselves as helpless slaves rather than conquering heroes.

In today's workplace there's much talk about the slave mentality, and employees commonly refer to themselves as wage slaves. These terms tend to conjure up images of worker drones in the lower realms of commerce. But everyone is vulnerable to the slave mentality. Whether you're a CEO or a sales clerk, if you see yourself only in terms of where you are at the moment, if you tend to resist new ideas or techniques, you're in the same mind-set the Israelites were.

When Fortune 500 business consultant Tom Drucker introduced me to the work of Rick Ross, I was struck by similarities between the so-called slave mentality and what Ross terms "the ladder of inference." According to Ross, we perceive daily events through a filter of old beliefs and past experiences. There's no way to avoid doing this: "You can't live your life without adding meaning or drawing conclusions," he says. However, our personal filters often distort the events we see. The facts we choose to focus on may not be all that important, it's just that they reinforce what we already believe. At work, this results in our viewing new ideas through a thick lens of personal bias. We become enslaved by our established worldview.

Ross offers the following to illustrate the ladder of inference (my italics). The bottom rung of the ladder is always an actual event—observable data.

> 4. Mary can't keep up the pace, and so she's willing to have us lose our competitive edge. (*I draw conclusions from my assumptions.*)

> 3. She can't compete very well. (*I make assumptions based on my interpretation.*)

> 2. Mary doesn't like competition. (*I interpret her comment based on my personal beliefs and past experiences.*)

> 1. "We need to be less competitive," Mary says. "We need to find a way to reward people for the contribution they make as a whole." (*observable data*)

In the wilderness, it might have gone like this:

> 5. We will complain and rebel against Moses.

> 4. Moses brought us here to die.

> 3. Moses knows we'll die without water.

> 2. Without fresh water, we'll surly die.

> 1. There's no fresh water to drink.

Nowhere in the Book of Exodus do you find the Israelites pitching in and trying to locate water themselves. It's not because they're too weak; these are the very men who built Egypt's colossal monuments. They certainly had the physical ability to fend for themselves, but mentally they were helpless. When they were slaves, they were dependent upon their Egyptian masters for food, water, and shelter. In the desert, their old frame of reference proved impossible to shed.

How can managers and their staffs break out of the slave mentality? The answer, according to Ross, is to:

- become more aware of your own thinking and reasoning (*reflection*)
- make your thinking and reasoning more visible to others (*advocacy*)
- inquire into others' thinking and reasoning (*inquiry*)

Because the ladder of inference occurs in mere seconds, it takes a deliberate effort to stop and examine it. To do this, Ross suggests that you ask questions such as:

- What is the observable data?
- Does everyone agree on what the data is?
- Can you run me through your reasoning?

- How did we get from that data to these assumptions?
- When you said "(your inference)," did you mean "(my interpretation of it)"?

These questions compel you and your coworkers to *reflect* on the data, articulate (or, in Ross's terms, *advocate*) your reasoning, and *inquire* how your colleagues reached their assumptions. They pull you out of your normal frame of reference and show you a broader view.

As Moses attempted to transform his tribe of slaves into a free nation, he used two of these techniques: advocacy and inquiry. (Reflection might not have been high on his agenda, since his mission was clear and coming straight from God's mouth.) To complete his mission—the survival of the Israelites—Moses had to shift their paradigm from "we are slaves" to "we are free human beings."

In advocating this shift, he made his thinking visible by bringing his people the Ten Commandments. Moses emphasized their importance by creating rituals centered around the Tent of Meeting, where the Commandments were kept, and by frequently repeating the Lord's instructions. But Moses didn't simply pass along the word of God; he encouraged his people to discuss and debate the concepts. He appointed judges and magistrates to reflect on the new laws and settle disputes among the people—the tradition of inquiry that is still fundamental to Jewish thought. "Hear out your fellow man...low and high alike," Moses urged the Israelites.

Not all of the Israelites were able to make the shift. Somewhere along the line Moses saw that most of them would not be capable of self-determination. He made the decision to wander for forty years so he could enter Canaan with a new generation raised as free men and women. But some of the ex-slaves *did* make the leap; it was they who helped Moses teach the ways of freedom to that next generation. Then, as now, a paradigm shift couldn't be accomplished in one fell stroke. It had to trickle down. If your leadership style can cause a few key people to break through to a new way of perceiving themselves, they can transmit it down the ranks. Use reflection, advocacy, and inquiry to help make those breakthroughs happen.

11
Tell People the Rules and the Consequences of Breaking Them

THE BIBLE IS FULL OF RULES—THE "SHALTS" AND "SHALT nots" of the Ten Commandments and the scores of commands that support them. It also contains admonitions, detailed descriptions of what will befall the person who doesn't obey those rules. On Mount Sinai, after Moses recited a catalogue of rules for living and worshiping the Lord, he offered this warning in God's name: "If you follow My laws and faithfully observe My commandments...I will grant peace in the land and you shall lie down untroubled by anyone; I will give the land respite from vicious beasts , and no sword will cross your land. . . . I will look with favor upon you, and make you fertile and multiply you. . . . I will be ever present in your midst."

So far so good. But for those who stray, the punishment would be severe: "If you do not obey me and do not observe all these commandments . . . I will wreak misery upon you—consumption and fever, which cause the eyes to pine and the body to languish; you shall sow your seed to no purpose, for your enemies shall eat it. I will set My face against you: you shall be routed by your enemies, and your foes shall dominate you. You shall flee though none pursues. . . . I will spurn you."

Most managers shy away from telling employees that they will suffer consumption, fever, and paranoia if they don't follow the company policy manual. But too often, management is unclear about exactly what *will* happen if an employee fails to comply with a policy. There are rules in any workplace, whether or not they are clearly articulated. When people know the rules and the results of breaking them, they are in a better position to choose their actions.

Joe W. R. Lawson II, CEO of SESCO Management Consultants in Bristol, Tennessee, has spent thirty-seven years working with companies large and small in developing and implementing labor policies.

The author of two books on personnel policies, Lawson observes that the laws from Mount Sinai can be profound rules of living, working, and personal conduct. "The Old Testament makes it clear that if one wants to live happily in any community or organization, one must comply with the rules," he says. "Otherwise, he will be excluded." In a sense, then, the Bible was the original policy and procedure manual.

Unlike the Ten Commandments, however, your company's policy manual is not written in stone. In reality, even the Commandments were subject to commentary. For example, the prohibition against killing is mitigated in a case of self-defense. Similarly, your policies can be updated to deal with changing circumstances or staff profiles. Lawson recalled the case of a nursing home manager who was troubled by the number of paid sick days certain nurses were taking. She didn't believe the nurses were really sick. Rather than confront them with her suspicions (which were unprovable anyway), she came up with a new policy: bonus days for perfect attendance. If a nurse accumulated a certain number of days without being absent or tardy, he or she would get a bonus day off, with no excuse needed.

When the manager first introduced this policy, the employees resisted it. Soon, however, they saw its advantages—they could now take a day off when they needed, without having to lie and pretend they were sick. Lawson points out, "When they first heard the Ten Commandments, the Children of Israel didn't like the new rules. They felt Moses was trying to dictate to them that they had to live by standards they didn't agree with. But after they lived with those rules, they found they were living more happily, harmoniously, and enjoyably day to day. Similarly, the nurses found that they had more satisfaction and peace of mind with this new policy."

Every organization must have guidelines for people management, business ethics, teamwork, and customer service. These guidelines and the consequences of breaking them must be unequivocally stated. In our climate of moral relativity, one cynic claimed that had Moses descended the mountain in the 1990s, he would have come down with the Ten Suggestions! According to Lawson, "Every successful company I've worked with in my thirty-seven years as a management consultant has had written, published, distributed standards of performance"—standards, not suggestions.

If your company's policies are unspoken or ambiguous, you can't expect your staff to comply with them. Instead, you'll have to settle every problem individually—a tremendous waste of your time. Clear policies and procedures, issued in written form to each staff member, relieve a manager from playing Solomon. Ideally, we can imbue our organization's policies with some of the wisdom and respect for others that characterize the rules Moses brought down from Mount Sinai three thousand years ago.

12
Give Appropriate Reproof—and Learn to Take It

CONSTANT CRITICISM IS A DESTRUCTIVE WEAPON, BUT failure to criticize can be devastating as well. Moses understood that when you don't reprove someone who has done something wrong, the problem is likely to fester. Brewing resentments undermine the good of the community, so Moses laid down guidelines for dealing with those who misbehave: "You shall not hate your brother in your heart; you shall reprove your fellow and not bear a sin because of him. You shall not take revenge and you shall not bear a grudge against the members of your people; you shall love your fellow as yourself." Given the choice between taking negative feedback in the moment and being ambushed unawares by someone's long-simmering resentment, most people would prefer to take their lumps in the beginning. That is why it is vital to give people prompt feedback about their actions.

Giving reproof serves both you and the person you reprove. It serves you because it spares you from the pent-up anger and bitterness that come from not communicating. It also helps the other individual because it gives him or her the opportunity to see a problem behavior and change it. Your subordinate's annoying habit or costly error may be obvious to you but not to him. By offering feedback in a nonthreatening way, you give this person the tools to improve.

Note that the verse says, "Reprove your fellow." It does not say to berate him, humiliate him, or remind him daily of his past blunders. When you give reproof, try to do so without anger or blame. If you are feeling angry, wait until the most intense feeling passes before you speak. Give your feedback when you can honestly say that you are offering this input as a service to the other person. As Nathaniel Branden asserts in his book *Self-Esteem at Work*, "If someone does unacceptable work or makes a bad decision, do not limit yourself to corrective feedback. Invite an exploration of what made

the error possible, thus raising the level of conscious-
ness and minimizing the likelihood of a repetition."

The inability to get honest negative feedback is a
serious problem for many managers. Diana Peterson-
More, president of the Organizational Effectiveness
Group in Pasadena, California, does executive coaching
and mediation for corporations nationwide. She points
out that people in positions of power often do not get
honest feedback from their subordinates. "People agree
with them all the time, and they don't think that they're
getting all this agreement because subordinates are
afraid they'll lose their job if they disagree. Instead,
they start to think that they're doing everything right."
This power-blindness is difficult to overcome. One way
to ensure that you get the feedback you need is to make
a pact with another manager at your level to tell each
other the truth, no matter how painful. Another way is
to conduct a 360-degree performance review within
your organization, wherein everyone gets feedback
from all sides—subordinates, superiors, and peers.

Another rather novel approach is to let your staff
evaluate you. Lou Hoffman, the owner of a Silicon
Valley public-relations firm, felt it was important to
have someone tell him how he was doing. He realized
that just because he was the boss didn't mean he was
above the need for an annual review. In the spring of

1995, Hoffman hired consultant Allison E. Hopkins to conduct confidential employee interviews and give him a report card that he promised to share with his staff. Hoffman's employees were generally positive but gave him low ratings on his internal communications skills. "My first review was not a real pleasant experience," says Hoffman. "But you get over it." In fact, he now feels that the reviews have contributed greatly to his success. His company of forty-one employees posted $3.6 million in sales revenue last year; Hoffman believes he could not have reached it without the critiques: "I would likely have missed some of the early warning signs of problems." The $7,500 he spent on the process this year is worth every penny, he says.

Of course, Moses did not recommend giving reproof as a means of maximizing profits or streamlining organizations. He recommended it because of the underlying principle that all human beings are responsible for one another, so if we see someone making a mistake, we have a moral obligation to help correct it. If that person doesn't want to correct it, that's his or her choice. Whether giving or receiving a critique, remember that the spirit of love and service must dominate the dialogue. If either one of you comes away feeling more angry, more vengeful, or resentful, then something went awry in the process and you will need to try again. As Moses said, "You shall reprove your fellow...and you shall not bear a grudge...you shall love your fellow as yourself." Give criticism in the manner that you yourself would find easy to take, and your colleague will probably be able to take it as well.

13
Don't Take the
Lord's Name in Vain

THE THIRD COMMANDMENT—"THOU SHALT NOT TAKE
the name of the Lord thy God in vain"—may seem to
modern ears less significant than the other Commandments. Murder and adultery are more heinous sins, and
honoring thy mother and father a more sacred duty.
But I believe Moses, and certainly God, recognized the
extraordinary power language holds over the human
spirit. The Third Commandment confirms this power.

The goal of the Ten Commandments was to ele-
vate people to a more divine level. Moses taught the
Israelites that what works in the animal world—
killing, wanton sexuality, thievery—is not acceptable
for human beings. We must rise above those base

instincts, but it doesn't happen in a single grand gesture. Elevating oneself happens slowly, day by day, in our small interactions with one another.

To make the point that small actions often matter more than large ones, many ministers and rabbis tell the story of two people running a long-distance race. One runner's path is blocked by boulders, the other's is smooth and straight. The man with the smooth path has small pebbles in his shoes, which constantly aggravate him. Although his terrain is easier, the man with the pebbles in his shoes loses the race.

Those pebbles can be compared to the small insults and profanity that diminish our respect for one another. Profanity isn't a violent blow so much as a constant, demoralizing affront to our dignity. The term *blasphemy* comes closest to describing what is actually happening when we use vile language: It is defined as "irreverence toward something considered sacred or inviolable." We are all created in God's image, so when we diminish another person by using profanity, we diminish God. This is disrespect on a profound level—a level that merits inclusion in the Ten Commandments.

Because it's so prevalent in the media, there is a widespread sense that coarse language isn't terribly harmful. But it is. It wears people down, just as positive, respectful speech elevates them. No manager, schoolteacher, or parent should underestimate the power of language, as the following story related by labor expert Joe Lawson illustrates.

The case involved a Virginia retail firm that had about twenty-five employees. It had been in business for fifty years and was being run by a father-and-son team. "The problem happened when the employees became very dissatisfied and frustrated with how the company was communicating with them," recalled Lawson. The staff, which consisted of both whites and African-Americans, deeply resented the profanity supervisors used when addressing them. It was particularly distressing when it happened in front of customers.

"They showed no respect for the work of the employees," said Lawson. "This was the son—probably modeling his behavior after his father. Many of these employees had been there for years. They got out a piece of paper and wrote down their frustrations in a six-point letter to the owner—the father. All points had to do with how they were being treated on a daily basis: verbal abuse, profanity, and a lack of respect and appreciation. Not a single complaint had to do with wanting more or better benefits, nothing with safety on the job. It was signed by every employee."

When the workers presented their petition to the son, he refused to meet with them. The father did the same. "They were so frustrated they walked off the job," recounted Lawson. "They went to a local union hall and described their job dissatisfactions to a union business agent. It was a union-free shop until then." Soon the workers joined the union, and the firm brought in Lawson to help negotiate new wages and working conditions. When he looked at the union proposal, the first item on it was "No profanity allowed."

"I asked the union agent why this was included, and he said, 'It's one of the major reasons I'm across the table from you today.' Those labor negotiations lasted over six months. Fundamental nonmonetary considerations were at the root—dignity, respect." Ultimately, the employees won out.

Any parent knows the value of speaking respectfully and the fallout that results when we don't. There are few things as disheartening as hearing curses fly from our children's lips. We demand a higher level of conduct from them, and we should demand it of ourselves as well. Our colleagues, employees, and competitors are listening.

14
Show Your Connection
with the People

MOSES' FIRST ATTEMPT TO RALLY THE CHILDREN OF Israel was not a wild success. The Lord had urged him, "Say therefore to the Israelite people: 'I am the Lord. I will free you from the labors of the Egyptians....But when Moses told this to the Israelites they would not listen to Moses, their spirits crushed by cruel bondage." God then ordered Moses to tell Pharaoh to free the Israelites. At that, Moses balked. "The Israelites would not listen to me," he objected, "how then should Pharaoh heed me?"

The text then takes what appears to be a complete left turn. Instead of God responding to Moses, we read, "These were the heads of their father's houses," and the next fourteen verses trace the genealogy of Moses and Aaron from the time of Jacob forward. The passage ends with, "It was they who spoke to Pharaoh king of Egypt about bringing out the people of Israel from Egypt, this Moses and this Aaron."

The reader already knows that this is the Moses and Aaron who spoke to Pharaoh. Anyone who's been following the story from the beginning also knows the family background of Moses and Aaron. So why repeat it, and why repeat it here? One explanation is that multiple writers worked on the Bible, and many elements get repeated. That could be, but I believe in this case the review of Moses' background was intentional. In the verses that precede this, Moses had just made his first announcement to the Children of Israel—and it had fallen flat. The people ignored him. Moses then had a crisis of confidence and went back to God, saying, in effect, "Help! No one is taking me seriously." God simply repeated His instructions— and reviewed the family tree.

The lineage reinforces the sense of connection between Moses and the Children of Israel. Imagine the scene from their perspective: a stranger who's been raised in Pharaoh's palace comes to them and says, "Hey, I'm one of you and I'm going to rescue you!" A certain skepticism is not surprising. By reviewing

Moses' connection with the Hebrew people dating back to the time before they entered Egypt, the biblical author reaffirms that Moses really was a member of the tribe.

When you are the new manager, the rank and file may greet you with skepticism, sometimes even with animosity, as the Children of Israel did to Moses. They may ask, "Who are you? Where did you come from? What makes you think you can make our lives any easier?" They know—or at least they think they know—that you, as the new boss, have not walked in their shoes.

You can prove your connection to your staff in several ways, as Moses did. First, you can make sure they know all your qualifications for the job. Don't assume they've heard it through the grapevine—tell them yourself. Second, let them know what roots you share with them, even if you have progressed far beyond those roots. Lee Iacocca frequently reminded his employees of his own working-class background, and this is what Moses did when he reminded the Children of Israel about his long connection with the Jewish people. Finally, you must produce results. Moses had the advantage of being able to generate miracles, but even if you don't have a magic rod that you can use to part the Red Sea, you can win credibility by demonstrating that you're not afraid to get your hands dirty and that you are capable of doing the job.

Perhaps one of the most potent means of creating a bond between yourself and your staff is to show that you are willing to sacrifice something of value for their benefit. Jerry Danziger, vice chairman of Hubbard Broadcasting Corporation, recalls that early in his career in television, he had a manager who brought together a few of his top salesmen and said, "If you all meet the sales goal we've set today, I'll buy every one of you a Cadillac." Danziger remembers, "This was during the 1950s, and that car was something we really wanted. We met the goal. Then our manager came to us and said, 'Look, a lot of people worked to help the company meet this goal, and we've made a lot of profit. What if we share those profits with everyone in the company?' He still bought us our Cadillacs, but he also gave a part of the profits to everyone who had helped produce them. He built a huge amount of loyalty that way, because everyone knew that he could have kept those profits for the company, or for himself and the top level of managers, but instead he gave some of it to everyone." This story has often been repeated in the booming internet companies of the 1990s, where workers at every level received bonuses in company stock that skyrocketed in value.

Self-sacrifice can mean sharing the wealth, as Jerry Danziger's boss did, or sharing the work, as when you come in on a Saturday to help your staff take inventory. The ancient Chinese philosopher Lao-tzu alluded to the importance of self-sacrifice in leaders when he wrote: "Be gentle and you can be bold; be frugal and you can be liberal; avoid putting yourself before others and you can become a leader among men."

The list of qualifications Moses had was impressive: a good family history, education in the finest schools in Egypt, access to Pharaoh, and knowledge of his court. His pedigree included being a descendant of the tribe of Levi and a child of Hebrew slaves. People needed to know that about him from the beginning so that they would rally to his cause sooner rather than later. Ultimately, of course, he had to deliver results. He had to prove through his deeds that he deserved their trust and loyalty. You too will be judged by the results you get, but success will come easier if you first establish a connection with the people you hope to lead.

15
Beware the Mischief
of Misinterpretation

Sometimes we hear "information" that is actually a few notches off from the original intent. Biblical commentators have referred to this as "the mischief of miscommunication," a lighthearted term for what can, unfortunately, have serious consequences. Take the passage in the Bible where Moses returns from Mount Sinai with the second set of tablets: "As Moses came down from the mountain bearing the two tablets of the pact, Moses was not aware that the skin of his face was radiant, since he had spoken with Him [God]. Aaron and all the Israelites saw that the skin of Moses' face was radiant, and they shrank from coming near him."

As Moses approached the people, rays of light were emanating from his face. The Hebrew word for *ray* is *keren.* When the Bible was translated into Latin, this word was mistranslated as *horn.* In Hebrew, *keren* can mean either *ray* or *horn,* depending on the context. Here, it clearly meant ray. People who read the Latin version of the Bible assumed that Moses had horns. Even Michelangelo's great sculpture of Moses depicts him with horns. Over the centuries, this led to the absurd notion that Moses' descendants, the Jewish people, had horns as well.

As a manager or CEO, there is no getting around the fact that your words will be scrutinized by all who hear them. Today, perhaps more than at any other time, the typical workforce consists of people with various educational and cultural backgrounds. English is a second language for many of them. The way you converse with these employees and colleagues will have a dramatic impact on their working relationship with you. No matter how deeply some people may resent having to watch their language more carefully than they would, say, around their dinner table, the situation has more to do with social realities than political correctness. If you're not sensitive to the way you use the language, you can unintentionally hurt people's feelings, and that can have consequences all out of proportion to the "crime."

In January 1999, David Howard, a top aide of Washington, D.C., mayor Anthony A. Williams, was discussing an emergency fund with three staff members—two black, one white. He said, "We'll have to be niggardly with this fund because it's not going to be a lot of money." One of the men misunderstood the word *niggardly*, which means miserly, and took it as a racial epithet. Apparently, a lot of people to whom he recounted the incident also misunderstood the word. The episode quickly escalated into high drama— Howard offered his resignation, Williams accepted it, then Williams was blasted for caving in to ignorance and political correctness. Eventually he asked Howard to rejoin his staff, which the latter did, albeit in a different position. David Howard acknowledged that the incident gave him "a certain awareness" he had lacked before.

The extreme reaction to David Howard's use of *niggardly* might be enough to make the most confident manager paranoid, but that's not my intent. I only bring up this incident to point out the tremendous power language has always held over us, and why it's so important for a leader to choose his or her words with care. Some commentators speculate that this might explain why God chose Moses, who was "slow of speech and tongue," to lead the Israelites. Moses had to think carefully before he spoke, since speech was difficult for him. Aaron delivered most of God's edicts, but when Moses himself spoke, it was very, very deliberately. Fewer mistakes are made that way, with fewer opportunities for misunderstanding.

As a manager, you have to be careful not only how you speak but also how you listen. Every tale has two sides, and every story has a context. As the leader, you'll often be called upon to referee arguments or dole out demerits for misconduct. When doing so, remember a story that's a favorite among my colleagues: One day, two congregants came to the rabbi's house to ask his help in settling a dispute. All the while, the rabbi's wife was eavesdropping at the door. The first man told his version of the story to the rabbi, who listened thoughtfully. At the end of the man's monologue, the rabbi said, "You know, you're right." Then he listened to the second man. At the end of his story, the rabbi said, "You know, you're right." As soon as the two men left, his wife opened the door and confronted him: "You must be crazy! You just told both of those men they were right. They can't both be right." The rabbi looked at her and said, "You know, *you're* right."

In many cases, both parties have a justifiable point, and it's your job to make a judgment call. You must lis-

ten carefully to all sides without jumping to conclusions, get the story clearly, and get it in context. Over
the years I've come to rely on other people to help me
out in this regard. If the information I'm receiving
seems overly complex or somehow off base, I ask the
opinion of one or two trusted friends. We all have at
least a few biases that will cause us to misinterpret
information. The most we can hope for is to know our
own weaknesses and compensate for them by asking
the opinion of others.

When you fail to listen carefully, things can go
wrong in a big way. In April 1985, Coca-Cola decided
to replace its traditional formula with a new one that
was sweeter and lacked the "sting" of the original. By
that July, amid an uproar from dissatisfied consumers,
the company reintroduced the original Coke as Coke
Classic. By October, Coke Classic was outselling New
Coke by as much as six to one. New Coke was a dud.

Coca-Cola had conducted $4 million dollars'
worth of market studies and taste tests before deciding
to tamper with the soft drink's secret formula. Obviously they misinterpreted the results of those tests.
Executives at the company later admitted they under-
estimated the intensity of Americans' love of the original formula. Whether it was nostalgia or simply a
matter of taste, people preferred the old Coke, and the

company didn't get the message until too late. Even $10 million in advertising couldn't alter the fate of New Coke. Today it's merely a memory, while Coca-Cola Classic lives on.

The mischief of misinterpretation can trip you up anywhere. Get in the habit of paying attention to your own words and listening carefully to the words of others, and you'll have a better chance of keeping the mischief to a minimum.

LEADING
IN THE WILDERNESS

Moses faced tremendous challenges during the forty years he and his people spent in the wilderness. There were logistical problems: He had to keep the ill-prepared Israelites alive in the harshest of territories, where food, water, and shelter were always scarce. There were motivational obstacles: The former slaves were terrified and unable to care for themselves, and at every crisis they turned on their leader.

Alert to the strengths and limitations of his group, Moses constantly searched for ways to motivate and inspire them. When there was a setback, he conferred with God, took a deep breath, and started again. Each crisis presented an opportunity to try out new practices, develop more sensitive laws for human interaction, or otherwise encourage his group to honor God and follow the path He had set for them. Moses sought out and nourished the brightest students and, when necessary, eliminated those who endangered the group. Although he was often frustrated with the Israelites, he never gave up on them. He was determined to teach his people how to live as free, self-governing men and women under God's law.

Part Two contains the most important lessons Moses has to offer about perseverance, creative problem-solving, and turning a disparate group of under-achievers into a forceful, passionate team.

16
Know the Turf

EVEN CASUAL READERS OF THE BIBLE NOTICE ONE THING right off: The Children of Israel were extraordinary kvetches. Their complaints are duly recorded from Exodus through Deuteronomy. But after all, they were ex-slaves and had endured an existence that's hard for modern readers to imagine. At the beginning of Exodus, the Bible reports that the Egyptians "made life bitter for [the Israelites] with harsh labor at mortar and bricks and with all sorts of tasks in the field." Those brief words fall short of revealing the horror that historically has been a slave's lot. As biblical commentator Jonathan Kirsch points out, the "harsh labor" was a form of genocide—the Egyptians planned to work the Israelites to death to keep their population down. Kirsch likens the life to that of prisoners in

Nazi concentration camps. After generations of such bondage, the Hebrews were in many respects a broken people. It's no surprise that as soon as they left Egypt, they began to crumble.

With a group this fragile, Moses had to radiate utter confidence: *Of course* they would make it to the Promised Land; they would survive, no matter how barren the desert. They would transform themselves from slaves to freemen. God had decreed it.

Moses was able to radiate this confidence because whenever a crisis erupted, he found a solution. When the thirsty and exhausted Israelites arrived at a spring of bitter water, Moses tossed some herbs into it, "and the water became sweet." Moses next led them to Elim, where there were "twelve springs of water and seventy palms." When they complained of hunger, Moses told them, "By evening you shall eat flesh, and in the morning you shall have your fill of bread." Low-flying quail filled the skies that night, and the next morning manna covered the ground.

How could he be so resourceful? Moses knew the turf. During his years as a nomadic shepherd, he had learned the ways of the desert. Desert tribes knew how to make brackish water drinkable by adding certain herbs. They knew about manna, too—to this day Bedouins, nomads of the Sinai Peninsula, eat what may be the very same substance, produced by insects that extract, then excrete, the sap from desert shrubs. Like biblical manna, the sap hardens at night and dissolves at dawn. The Bedouins call the food *mann*.

While the Sinai might have been a frightening wilderness to the Israelites, it was formidable but not daunting to Moses, who had lived there as a shepherd for many years. He didn't just stumble across fresh springs, he knew their locations. When he found manna or turned bitter water sweet, Moses credited God, but whether it was God's hand or Moses' resourcefulness, the result was the same: Moses' knowledge of the turf gave the people confidence—it seemed preordained that although they might suffer, they would eventually prevail. Moses passed his survival skills on to them and they transformed themselves.

Few businesses today are immune to sudden changes. A staff that's been thrown into the maw of restructuring will often react like the Hebrew slaves: "You have brought us out into this wilderness to starve to death!" They'll be vulnerable and frightened, looking to their leader for direction and confidence. To supply it, you must know the turf you'll be traveling. Or, as Barry Sternlicht, chairman and CEO of Starwood Hotels and Resorts, once told me in connection with his attempt to merge two distinct hotel chains,

Sheraton and Westin, "Before you can steer the ship, you have to understand the ship."

If you haven't crossed the territory before, there are ways to make up for lost time. That's what Jane Bevan, as public-relations manager, did when she was put in charge of overhauling the internal communications of Britain's Natural History Museum. Founded in the 1700s, the museum had grown to encompass fourteen acres in central London, with a staff of 756. Each department was rigidly divided according to specialty and rank, with communication discouraged among departments and even among workers in the same department. A May 1997 article in *People Management* interviewed Bevan, who recalled that "there was a lot of intellectual snobbery and grade snobbery" among employees. Dr. Rob Huxely, head curator in the botany department, concurred: "Traditionally, junior members of the staff weren't allowed to cross the herbarium during working hours. Woe betide the junior fern curator who was found in lichens."

By 1990 this antiquated structure was taking a toll on the museum. While the rest of the world developed Web sites and vast databases, the museum and its tremendous resources remained stuck in the nineteenth century. Management decided to completely restructure the museum to consolidate its strengths.

"Job cuts were achieved through early retirements," the article reports, but "the traditional system of isolated, semi-autonomous, hierarchical departments had been deeply embedded, and many employees felt betrayed and insecure."

Jane Bevan's task was to teach these insulated, skeptical employees how to communicate openly with one another. But as a newcomer to the museum, Jane herself was unclear about the turf. What were the attitudes at all levels of the organization? Where were the land mines, the oases? To find out, she implemented a museum-wide employee-attitude survey. Its results would give her a map of the territory into which she was heading.

The survey provided Bevan with the lay of the land. She found out which programs managers would support, and which would be more difficult to implement. She learned what the employees held dear and what they viewed with suspicion. Points of contention between management and support staff appeared in bold relief. Based on the survey, Bevan laid out a strategy for revamping the internal communications system. A company newsletter, training programs, suggestion schemes, and information hot spots were created or revised. An intranet computer system was set up. One major milestone was the publication of an internal business directory that listed for the first time the names, projects, and special skills of all employees.

Only by knowing the turf could Bevan have succeeded in leading such an isolated and traumatized group into the information-swapping culture of the 1990s. The turf in this case was the attitudes of the employees themselves, who mistrusted one another, management, and the whole concept of sharing information. If she had simply swooped down on the staff with a cartonful of intranet software, Bevan's efforts might have badly misfired.

Knowing the turf gives you the power to make wise decisions, lead with confidence, and empower others. Moses taught his people the skills they needed to survive in the desert, and Jane Bevan taught the staff at the Natural History Museum that communication was liberating, not threatening. When you know the turf, you too can teach your staff how to transform themselves into survivors.

17
Recognize When the
Roundabout Way Is Best

THE YEARS MOSES SPENT WANDERING IN THE DESERT ARE misunderstood by a great many people. His route was purposeful, and there was never any question of being lost. From the outset God saw that the Israelites weren't ready for an aggressive itinerary: "God did not lead them by way of the land of the Philistines, although it was nearer; for God said, 'The people may have a change of heart when they see war, and return to Egypt.' So God led the people roundabout, by way of the wilderness at the Sea of Reeds."

The distance between Egypt and Canaan isn't great; I've driven it myself in a few hours. But the psychological distance the Israelites had to travel before they were capable of conquering Canaan was a much longer trip.

By the time Moses shepherded the former slaves to Mount Sinai, it was clear they weren't ready to accept the Ten Commandments, much less challenge the inhabitants of Canaan. As it turned out, the group that left Egypt would never be ready. Moses took the Israelites the way they needed to go to grow. It took forty years to raise a tough new generation, forty years to prove to themselves that they were capable of taking their Promised Land.

Sometimes it's more important to prove that a task can be done well than to do it quickly. To outsiders it may seem slow or circuitous, but outsiders don't know your staff. You alone are aware of their abilities and weaknesses. If Moses had led the Israelites into the Promised Land as disorganized and poorly motivated as they were, they would have failed miserably.

When the space shuttle *Challenger* exploded after takeoff on January 28, 1986, the behind-the-scenes scramble that had preceded the launch was reported everywhere. The spacecraft carried Christa McAuliffe, the first astronaut in the much-publicized Teacher-in-Space Program. In his state-of-the-union address, to be delivered the evening of the launch, President Ronald Reagan planned to devote three paragraphs to

McAuliffe and the program. Political pressure to get the shuttle off the ground had led NASA to disregard the warnings of scientists who were concerned about the spacecraft's O-rings. There was too much pressure to get the job done, and not enough will to get it done right. The roundabout way—waiting until the weather was optimal and fixing the O-rings—would have skirted the tragedy.

When I interviewed Sherry Lansing, chairman of Paramount Pictures' Motion Picture Group, I was surprised to learn of the serendipitous route her career had taken. Lansing, the first female head of a major motion picture studio, is widely heralded as the patron saint of women in the film business. "I knew I wanted to be in the movies," she told me, but when she first got started in the 1970s, the industry was mostly a boys' club. Lansing, a teacher, decided to try acting, "because that was all I knew a woman could do in film. But I didn't like it—I felt very uncomfortable. I didn't know how to be anybody other than myself." She began asking people on the set about their jobs. "I never had a master plan," she says cheerfully. "I never said, 'I want to produce movies,' or, 'One day I will be head of this studio.'"

Instead, Lansing followed her interests wherever they led. She got out of acting and began reading scripts. From then on, "Each step was exciting in and of itself. Each job seemed like heaven, and I didn't really have the next goal. When I was promoted to vice president of creative affairs, that meant you read the material and actually got to work with the writers. Then I became vice president of production, which meant you actually got to work on the production. Then I became head of production, then head of 20th Century-Fox."

Far from being the driven businesswoman with a dream to rise to the top of a competitive industry, Lansing always focused on the moment. "I often say, 'Just trying is worthy of respect. Just trying to write a book is great. Just getting up to bat is great. Enjoy the process, and don't worry about being a success.'"

In real life, business is not a straight path but a series of ups and downs, cyclical like the seasons. With any endeavor there are numerous influences that might change one's original route. Fluctuations in the market, the political scene, overseas economies, and even the weather might mean that waiting or regrouping will ultimately get you there faster than charging ahead.

Entrepreneur Skip Lane took a path that mean-dered, doubled back on itself, and ultimately reached the right destination. Directly out of school, Lane signed on with Cable & Wireless PLC, a London-based telecommunications company. In an interview with *The Wall Street Journal* (June 22, 1998), he recalled: "With the company going through lots of changes and growth, I decided that I could do the same thing—at twenty-four years of age—and get married in the same year. So I decided to start a long-distance resale company. I quickly realized that I was going to need three times as much money, three times the expertise, three times the experience, and about twelve times the luck."

A year and a half later, Lane merged his company with a larger one that had the experience, money, and customer base he needed. But at the time of the merger, he found out his new company would itself be merging with ITT.

"I didn't want to work with ITT," Lane stated. So he went back to Cable & Wireless, "to get more education and more experience in the business world." For seven years he learned the ropes in sales and development. Finally, although he was earning an excellent salary, Lane quit Cable & Wireless to try building his own company again. In June 1992, he founded Network One. No longer an eager but inexperienced twenty-something, he now had the savvy to make his business a success. Today the company employs more than sixty people.

As much as our society prizes the can-do, bluff-your-way-through-anything spirit, people like Sherry Lansing and Skip Lane show us that faster is not always wiser. If your "wandering" makes you stronger, smarter, and better equipped for the future, you are on the right path.

18
Give Talented People Room to Shine

"GOD IS IN THE DETAILS," ARCHITECT LUDWIG MIES VAN der Rohe liked to say, paraphrasing a sentiment first broached in the Old Testament. As Moses found out, God is also *into* details. His specifications for building the Tent of Meeting cover all sorts of minutiae, down to the altar utensils and the design of Aaron's robe ("The opening for the head shall be in the middle of it"). Moses served as contractor for the construction of the Tent, Holy Ark, altars, sacramental garments, and vessels. He needed to find a crew that would do the job perfectly, to the standards of this most exacting client. Fortunately, he had an advantage most managers lack: God Himself told him whom to hire.

"See, I have singled out by name Bezalel...I have endowed him with a divine spirit of skill, ability, and knowledge in every kind of craft; to make designs for work in gold, silver, and copper, to cut stones for setting and to carve wood." God also assigned Bezalel an assistant, Oholiab, and a team of skilled craftsmen to complete the project.

While we read extensive—even laborious—descriptions of exactly how each piece of the Ark must be constructed, there is no record of Moses demanding progress reports, hanging around the construction site to make sure everything is going according to plan, or even repeating his instructions to Bezalel. He knew he had the right person for the job, and he let that person do his job without interference.

Wise managers know that talents such as Bezalel do their best work when they are given creative space and are not expected to justify every decision. One of the myths that Warren Bennis and Burt Nanus dispel is that "the leader controls, directs, prods, manipulates. This is perhaps the most damaging myth of all." Bennis stresses time and again that leadership is not so much the exercise of power itself as the empowerment of others.

Nathaniel Branden echoes this belief in his book *Self-Esteem at Work.* "Aim your people—and get out of the way," he writes. "Let them know you are available if needed but do not impose your presence or involvement gratuitously. Remember your business is to inspire, coach, and facilitate....Remember that the measure of your success is their creative self-assertiveness."

Even the savviest manager can forget this fundamental rule and micromanage his or her staff to distraction. An entertainment attorney told a story about how one of the industry's most brilliant innovators fell into the micromanagement trap when he was president of a fledgling television network. A client of the attorney's was premiering the first show on the network, but progress was dragging because the CEO hadn't yet approved the look of the set. The pressure was enormous, as all eyes were on the man who had dared to compete with the other networks. Finally, the attorney arranged to meet the CEO for lunch at the studio commissary. While they were eating, he reached into his briefcase and pulled out a swatch of carpeting and one of drapery fabric.

"Listen, I have a question for you," he asked the CEO. "My wife and I are redecorating our living room. I wanted to know if you think this carpeting goes with this drape."

"You're accusing me of micromanaging, aren't you?" the CEO responded, and that was the end of it.

By throwing a little humor into the situation, the attorney was able to convince the CEO to step back long enough for the show to proceed.

A great many leaders fall prey to the temptation to micromanage, even though they know it can be counterproductive. Trust has much to do with this urge. If you trust that your employees share your commitment and vision, you're more likely to give them the room they need to shine. Moses could trust Bezalel because God had recommended him. Today's managers don't have the luxury of an Almighty seal of approval, but some have found that the trust equation works in reverse: the more room you give your employees, the more likely they are to share and promote your vision.

One of the most oft-repeated success stories is the invention of the Post-it note by 3M scientist Art Fry. Mr. Fry didn't invent the adhesive used on the Post-it, and he didn't invent the paper, but he did put the two together. His inspiration for Post-it notes dates back to the early 1970s, when he sang in his church choir and used scraps of paper to mark selections in his hymnal. Unfortunately, the paper kept falling out and he'd often lose his place. "I needed a bookmark that would stay put, yet could easily be removed without damaging my hymnal," Fry recalls.

Around the time Art Fry was thinking about how to make more cooperative bookmarks, his colleague Dr. Spencer Silver was doing basic research on adhesives. He'd come up with a low-tack adhesive that stuck lightly to many surfaces, yet remained sticky even after you repositioned it. Fry soon realized Spencer's adhesive was perfect for his needs. He applied some of the adhesive to the edge of a piece of paper, and *voilà:* a removable, reusable bookmark that wouldn't fall out.

Not long afterward, Fry realized his invention's full potential. He brought the idea to 3M's management, who provided him with a research team. Eighteen months later, they were ready to show samples to the marketing department.

The rest of the Post-it note story is history. What's not so widely known is that Art Fry's discovery was not entirely a lucky fluke. It was also the natural outcome of a 3M policy that encourages scientists to spend up to fifteen percent of their time working on projects they hold dear. Without the time and support to pursue his sticky bookmark, Art Fry's idea might have remained just that. The fifteen-percent policy has served 3M well, helping to foster other breakthrough products such as Scotch tape.

Would it have helped Art Fry to have management peering over his shoulder at every turn? Probably not.

As Sherry Lansing told me, "I don't believe in micro-managing. Once I've green-lit a project, I trust the film-makers and producers to do their jobs." Like Moses, the managers at 3M and Ms. Lansing know enough to give talented people the materials and personnel they need, and then keep out of their way.

19
Look for Symbols
of Strength

THE MOST ANCIENT SYMBOL OF THE JEWISH PEOPLE IS THE
menorah, the seven-branched candelabra that the craftsman Bezalel fashioned out of gold, "according to the
pattern that the Lord had shown Moses." Of all the
objects God directed the Israelites to create, it was this
candelabra that best reflected the spirit of the people.
The Star of David also represents Judaism, but the
menorah was there first. In the Roman catacombs, on
graves and sarcophagi, the image of the menorah is
etched. From the Exodus until today, it has remained
the most sacred symbol of the Jewish people.

The symbolism of light is important to many
faiths—the light of freedom against the darkness of

slavery, the light of hope against the blackness of despair. Yet the Israelites took it one step further. What was it about the menorah that made them embrace it not just as a part of their ritual but as the symbol of their very existence?

A clue can be found in the instructions God gave for creating the menorah. "You shall make a lampstand of pure gold," recounts the Bible. "The lampstand shall be made of hammered work; its base and its shaft, its cups, calyxes, and petals shall be of one piece." In the original Hebrew, the word that is used is *miksha*, which means *hardened*. By constantly beating the piece, Bezalel was hardening the design until it was perfect. The analogy for any group, and for the Jewish people through the ages, is that you're going to get beaten up a lot. You're going to be taking the blows of life, but by coming in and doing your daily work, you'll also be strengthening yourself and adding your light to the common effort.

Many people feel that simply coming in to work every day isn't contributing much, that there's no glory in it. In reality, coming in every day builds the momentum that makes a company strong. As a manager, it's up to you to remind your staff that no one's job is small or insignificant; everyone's performance contributes to the greater whole. When people accept this idea, the group coalesces and becomes more than the sum of its parts. And as Moses discovered, symbols are key to maintaining this feeling of unity over the long haul.

Moses' great achievement was to mold a group of frightened individuals into a unified nation. He took people who had been beaten down by slavery, by years in the desert, by the sin of the golden calf and other slides into unfaithfulness, and unified them by teaching the word of God. But Moses understood that they would also need a physical symbol of faith and endurance. God had decreed that the Israelites could not worship images of any person or animal, yet human beings do crave images to remind them of who they are and why they are on their journey. The menorah came to signify all that was essential about being a God-centered nation: survival, following the Lord's word, and bringing your light—your effort—to the common goal every day. Six of the candelabra's branches represented workdays, while the seventh represented the Sabbath, a day of rest. The concept of taking a day off each week to contemplate the Lord was a revolutionary one.

In business, too, symbols are valuable tools for inspiring people. I'm not referring to corporate logos or status symbols but to items that represent a shared experience that helped mold the organization. Even small symbols are uplifting: Many restaurants have the first dollar they earned pasted to the cash register, a symbol of their triumph in actually getting the place funded and open for business. Phil Blazer, founder of the *Jewish News Daily*, keeps an odd but inspiring symbol hanging on his office wall. Although it's a far cry from a golden candelabra, it's powerful just the same.

Phil's symbol of survival is a pair of black socks. They're famous among those who know him. These aren't just any socks, they're a particularly decrepit pair that Phil wore for eight days straight when he was desperately trying to meet the deadline on the *Daily's* first edition. He and his fledgling staff slept at the office, sweated twenty-hour days, and, after an unforgettably torturous week, got the paper to the printer on time. Then he framed his frayed and acrid socks. Now, whenever another difficult deadline looms, he has a staff meeting, points to the socks, and says, "Remember those days? We did it then, and we can do it now. We can meet this deadline."

We all need symbols to inspire us to go forward. It can be a humorous symbol of survival, like Phil's socks. It can be an award your staff has received for work done within the industry or the community. It might be a photograph of a group of staffers crossing the finish line at the annual Walk for Cancer or some other worthy event.

Like the menorah, the best symbols remind us of our strength. They signify an extraordinary challenge that demanded extraordinary effort. The best symbols are proof that here, on this spot, we all pulled together and shined. In your place of business, there may be such a symbol packed away on a back shelf or lying forgotten in a desk drawer. If so, dust it off and put it up on the wall. If your department survives an especially grueling experience, look for an object that can symbolize it. Symbols have an uncanny power to bind people together, so search them out and put their power to work for you.

20
Lead with a Team

THE NAME MOSES USUALLY EVOKES IMAGES OF A LONE figure towering over his flock, not quite a god but not merely mortal, either. When we look for examples of how a single human being can be a force for change in the world, we think of him. In art, Moses is pictured preaching to the Hebrew crowds, striding down Mount Sinai bearing the tablets, or standing alone, his staff raised before the cleft waters of the Red Sea. In the most famous image, Michelangelo's colossal sculpture entitled *Moses*, he is seated in a thronelike chair, his muscles bulging, his body tense, the tablets gripped under his arm. On his face is a look of darkening wrath intended for the stiff-necked Israelites, his errant "children."

Modern interpretations of Exodus have also focused on Moses' individual metamorphosis, casting him as a paradigm of personal growth. He is exiled to the desert, where he "individuates" and reemerges to find his mission and gain an identity. But neither the image of Moses the towering lawgiver nor that of Moses the fully actualized man shows us the reality: he was part of a team. Not even Moses could do it all alone.

In Exodus 9:1 and 10:1 we read "The Lord said to Moses, 'Come unto Pharaoh.'" Often these words are translated as "Go unto Pharaoh," but the accurate Hebrew translation is not *go* but *come*—as in "Come with me, with your brother Aaron, with the team we assemble." According to biblical commentators, God never intended that Moses act alone.

Who were the other members of "Team Moses"? At the beginning there was his mother, who had the courage to hide him from the Egyptian executioners, and his sister Miriam, who watched over his fragile basket as it drifted down the Nile and later was a powerful presence in the wilderness. The Egyptian princess who drew Moses from the river and raised him as her son in Pharaoh's court was also a key player.

Both of Moses' mothers crafted his identity. His Egyptian mother exposed him to the protocol of court, and that knowledge enabled him to gain entrée when he returned to demand that Pharaoh free the slaves. His natural mother, who nursed him, and his sister and brother, with whom he was undoubtedly in contact, taught him about his Hebrew identity. Contrary to the films *The Ten Commandments* and the more recent *Prince of Egypt*, the Bible never implies that Moses was raised believing he was Egyptian, only to discover the truth as an adult. Exodus matter-of-factly reports that "when Moses had grown up, he went out to his kinsfolk and witnessed their labor." Some scholars maintain that Moses might have been raised as a Semitic prince in Pharaoh's court by both his Egyptian and his natural mother—two early influential members of his team. This dual upbringing was crucial to his success.

Moses' brother Aaron was an indispensable part of the team. Without him, Moses, who was often "halting of speech," wouldn't have been an effective communicator. Aaron also gave Moses credibility among the slaves, who otherwise might have doubted the sincerity of this well-bred "prince." Later Aaron was put in charge of the priesthood, thus solidifying the rituals of the fledgling nation. The Bible makes it clear that Moses could not have achieved his mission without his brother's help.

Another extremely important member of Team Moses was his father-in-law, Jethro. When Moses was exiled, Jethro took him in, taught him desert survival skills, and gave him a flock to tend. Jethro also gave Moses his daughter Zipporah to wed. Under Jethro's guidance, Moses flowered into full manhood. When he was first attempting to lead the Children of Israel in the wilderness, it was Jethro who told him, "The task is too heavy for you; you cannot do it alone," and advised him to appoint magistrates and judges to help settle disputes. Jethro may have played an even more important role in Moses' development: some scholars believe that he taught Moses monotheism. So great was the respect the ancient sages had for the Midiianite priest Jethro that they named the portion of the Bible that contains the Ten Commandments "Yitro" after him.

Moses' wife Zipporah accompanied him through-out many years of exile and, in one memorable episode, saved his life. Moses' successor, Joshua, was a later addition to the team. Even the craftsman Bezalel can be considered a crucial member of Team Moses. Moses himself couldn't have carried out God's instruc-tions for building the Ark of the Covenant and the other ritual items for the sanctuary, all of which were necessary to give structure and focus to the new faith.

So Team Moses consisted of at least eight people: his natural mother, his adopted mother, his wife, sis-ter, brother, father-in-law, his successor Joshua, and the craftsman Bezalel. Some of these team members let him down: Aaron, when he allowed the Israelites to fashion a golden calf; Miriam, when she gossiped about his Cushite wife. Nevertheless, they were still part of his team. He fought with them, reconciled, and moved forward. In the final analysis, he depended upon them for emotional support, leadership support, and encouragement. They helped him mold the people.

This concept of team leadership is being embraced by the visionaries of our day. When I asked Bob Pittman, president of America Online, "Where do you think the leadership lies in a corporate infrastructure?" he replied, "I'm not a believer in the old military model of the general. I don't believe that in a big company you can have a leader and lots of helpers. What you really have is a team. We're all empowered. The way you run a big company is that the leader has to give pieces of it to someone else. [CEO] Steve Case has given me the day-to-day operation. I have taken that in turn and given pieces of it to other people.

"It's very dynamic. You're not taking the approach of, 'I'm higher in the organization than you are, therefore I have a better idea.' You are merely saying, 'I'm spending more of my time managing. I'm further away, but I have a broader view. You are spending more of your time specifically looking at an issue. You are going to know more about that.' It's having that sort of mutual respect that usually makes it work so well."

The Book of Exodus provides one particularly memorable image of Moses as a team player. As the Israelites travel from Egypt to Mount Sinai, they stop to camp at Rephidim. There, the Amalekites confront them. Moses orders his men to battle, assuring them that he will be standing on a nearby hill with the staff of God in his hand. "Whenever Moses held up his hand, Israel prevailed," says the Bible, "but whenever he let down his hand, Amalek prevailed. But Moses' hands grew heavy; so they took a stone and put it under him and he sat on it, while Aaron and Hur, one on each side, supported his hands; thus his hands remained steady until the sun set."

Israel triumphed in that battle. Whether you're weary or not, whether you realize it or not, we all need other people to support us and help us accomplish our objectives.

21
Anticipate the Future and Use It to Your Advantage

When Moses stood before Pharaoh and demanded, "Let my people go," he knew exactly what he was up against. The confrontation between the two leaders would spark a monumental clash of worldviews. Ancient Egyptians worshiped the sun god Ra, animals, the Nile and anything that came out of the Nile, yet they considered the lives of slaves to be nearly worthless. The God of Moses held that human beings were the most precious of all creatures, the "crown of creation." Moses had to prove to the Egyptians—on *their* terms—that his God was more powerful than all their deities. Until he did that, Pharaoh would never free the Children of Israel.

As it turned out, it took ten devastating plagues, each of which Moses predicted, to convince Pharaoh of the Lord's power. Because God's messenger, Moses, was able to foretell the plagues, Pharaoh was eventually convinced that God, not Ra, was the power behind them. But was Moses really foretelling the plagues, or was he simply paying attention? Having been chosen to lead this mission, Moses looked at the world with different eyes. He scrutinized the earth and sky, where he fully expected to see the Lord's wrath displayed until Pharaoh came around.

The first plague, turning the Nile to blood, may have in fact been a red tide. Some scholars believe that there were long expanses of time between the plagues and that Moses may have seen signs of an impending red tide, or noticed a cyclical pattern of red mud washing through from upstream, before he ever approached Pharaoh. If so, he would have known what was coming and could have accurately "predicted" this plague. What made Moses extraordinary, however, is the way he used a single piece of information to forecast events that would unfold weeks or months later. A red tide would disrupt the balance of life along the Nile, resulting in a huge increase in the frog population fleeing onto land. Moses noticed these developments and predicted the plague of frogs. He reasoned that when the frogs died, their bodies would be a breeding ground for lice and other insects, and he predicted the ensuing two plagues. So it went with each of the plagues that were natural disasters. Moses studied the forces around him, thought about their probable consequences, and made his predictions.

Even if you accept each plague as having been a self-contained disaster visited in sequence by God upon Egypt, the lesson is still valuable. You, as a manager, must be attuned to great upheavals as well as more subtle shifts in the market environment. It's not enough to notice that things are changing, or even to see around the next curve. Go further: Envision three or four consequences down the line.

In 1987, a young sales manager felt the winds of change rippling through his community. Greg Penske, then twenty-four, had taken over his father's used-car dealership at a time when the mostly white town of El Monte, California, was beginning to attract middle-class immigrants from many corners of the world. Some businesses responded with a backlash, pushing local government to enact a ban on non-English signs. They saw a threat; Penske saw an opening.

Rather than merely hiring a few Spanish- or Chinese-speaking salespeople to accommodate the immigrants, Penske aggressively pursued these new customers.

He placed ads in ethnic newspapers, radio, television—even a neighborhood Nigerian newsletter. He personally appeared, speaking a few lines of Mandarin, in an ad that ran on the local Chinese TV station. Other El Monte businesses targeted one or two immigrant communities. Penske's Longo Toyota tried to target all of them, eventually hiring a diverse staff that could sell cars in twenty languages, including Tagalog, Korean, Shanghainese, and Vietnamese.

By the end of 1997, Longo Toyota was the top-grossing car dealership in California, pulling in about $350 million a year. "A lot of people in business don't like change," Penske says. "I love change. I saw it coming and went after it."

When Moses returned to Egypt, he was alert to the changes that would signal God's power. He gazed more intently at the natural forces around him and thought more deeply about what he saw. Do the same with the forces that surround you. Think past the immediate event to the ripples it will cause tomorrow, next month, next year. Anticipate the future and use it to your advantage.

22
See Crisis
as an Opening Door

THE TENTH PLAGUE, IN WHICH THE LORD STRUCK DOWN the firstborn in every Egyptian household, was the final blow in a long series of disasters. The stress wrought by years of escalating crises can be heard in Pharaoh's parting plea to Moses: " 'Up, depart from among my people, you and the Israelites with you! Go, worship the Lord as you said! Take also your flocks and your herds, as you said, and be gone!' "

Before Moses returned to Egypt it would have been unthinkable for that mighty nation to relinquish six-hundred thousand slaves. The plagues made it possible. These catastrophes convinced the Egyptians that their world would keep disintegrating until the Israelites were freed. Egyptians suffered greatly during the plague years, losing their crops, their livestock, and their health. With each new affliction, they grew more despairing, more certain that the disasters would never end. No wonder that when Pharaoh finally freed the Israelites, "the Egyptians urged the people on, impatient to have them leave the country." By the time they had endured ten plagues, they were more than ready to consider the unthinkable. As for Pharaoh, his final words to Moses were, "And may you bring a blessing upon me also!" The king had become the supplicant, Moses the dispenser of blessings. In a crisis, everything can change.

Crisis, in fact, is sometimes the only door to change. Philips Electronics learned this the hard way. A pioneering manufacturer of audio, video, and recording equipment, Philips was on top of the world in the early 1980s. Its reputation for engineering was unequaled, its competitors few. Based in the Netherlands, Philips had regional managers in numerous locations throughout Europe. Each region was highly independent of the others, and each regional manager ran his division like a small kingdom.

Over the years, Philips employees came to understand that the key to lifelong job security was loyalty to individual managers and that personal relationships and

seniority mattered more than ability. According to Paul
Strebel, who reported on Philips in the May–June
1996 *Harvard Business Review*, "Position and power in
the company network determined who got what.…
[W]orkers had no incentive to work harder than people just above them…Philips had no effective mechanism for holding managers responsible.…[In] a culture
that encouraged loyalty over performance, no one was
able to challenge this mind-set effectively."

By 1990, the mind-set badly needed to be chal-
lenged. The economic scene had shifted dramatically;
now companies such as Sony and Panasonic were taking huge chunks of Philips's market. Two successive
CEOs had tried to make Philips more competitive, but
nothing worked. "Managers and subordinates were not
forced to understand how the changes essential to
turning the company around would require them to
take a fundamentally different view of their obliga-
tions." In other words, the changes were unthinkable
to Philips's employees.

Then Jan Timmer was put in charge. The first
thing he did was to officially label the situation a crisis.
Timmer brought Philips's top hundred managers to an
off-site retreat and handed each a sheet of paper. It
was a hypothetical press release announcing Philips's
bankruptcy. Timmer stated in no uncertain terms that

unless changes were made now, the press release would become reality. His managers had two choices: join him in his mission to entirely reshape the organization, or go elsewhere. "Operation Centurion had begun," writes Strebel, "and, with it, the end of life in the company as all those in the room had known it."

Operation Centurion instigated sweeping reforms throughout Philips. The way Timmer launched the program offers a lesson for all managers—sometimes it doesn't pay to soften a situation; sometimes calling a crisis by its true name is the only way to get people moving. Once a crisis is recognized for what it is, a spirit of open-mindedness—sparked by the primal urge to survive—replaces the old assumptions. Most people can rise to the challenge. In 1994 a company survey revealed that among Philips employees, "morale and feelings of empowerment had soared."

Rather than deny that a crisis exists, recognize it and use it. Serious crises visit organizations only rarely, but when they do, take advantage of the doors they can open.

23
Draw Out
Heartfelt Contributions

Moses' name—in Hebrew it means "to draw out"—has long been a source of inspiration to those familiar with his story. The metaphor is irresistible: Moses was drawn from the Nile River, and although he was raised as a prince, he would reject his luxurious surroundings in order to draw the Israelites out of Egypt. Moses had to arrange for their physical withdrawal from the "house of bondage" (which he did with the help of the plagues), but that was only the beginning. Once they were in the desert, Moses had to draw out their talents and commitment if the new nation was to survive.

No matter what team you're managing or what goal you've set your sights on, there are always two levels at work. The first, achieving the specific goal, is the easier. Move the people out of Egypt—done. Now that they're out, though, how do you get them to commit themselves to the greater mission, to feel fully invested in the cause? You've got their bodies; how do you get their hearts?

There's a lot of emphasis in the Bible on willing, heartfelt contribution. Listen to Moses' instructions for building the Tent of Meeting: "Take from among you gifts to the Lord; everyone whose heart so moves him shall bring them.... And let all among you who are skilled come and make all that the Lord has commanded." Exodus continues, "And everyone who excelled in ability and everyone whose spirit moved him came, bringing to the Lord his offering for the work of the Tent of Meeting.... All the men and women whose hearts moved them to bring anything... brought it as a freewill offering to the Lord."

More than being with the Lord in body, Moses wanted the Israelites to be with Him in spirit. He needed more than their contribution, he needed their freewill, heartfelt contribution. With that kind of passionate commitment, they would have a chance at survival. If they remained a group of escaped slaves whose hearts were back in Egypt, they would never make it.

Drawing out his people's commitment was Moses' lifelong, often frustrating, task. It's a daunting job for any manager, but the challenge is especially interesting in the nonprofit sector. As rabbi for several large congregations, I've learned a lot about drawing out the talents of volunteers. Unlike employees, volunteers come with a wide range of abilities, not all of which are especially useful for running a temple, at least not at first glance. Are their hearts in it? Certainly—they wouldn't be volunteering if they didn't want to help. But no one, no matter how good her intentions, feels truly part of a team unless she is offering her *best* talents to the cause. In matching volunteers to programs that make the most of their skills, I've discovered a basic rule: The better you know your people, the more possibilities you'll see.

The volunteer pool in many congregations consists of mothers—women in their twenties, thirties, and forties whose careers are often slowed or put aside during the years they're being full-time chauffeurs. At my temple in Miami, Florida, I made it a point to ask these women about their careers and backgrounds. As I got to know them, I realized that despite the mothers' higher education, their children were becoming much more knowledgeable than they about their faith. Many baby-boomer parents had long forgotten their own minimal religious training or had never had any in the first place. "I want my kids to know about our cultural heritage," they'd say, then shamefacedly admit that they themselves only came to worship on the high holy days.

Two of these "lapsed" mothers had been teachers in their lives before soccer and ballet shuttling, so I put Linda and Estelle on an education committee, hoping they'd bring some innovative ideas to the program. The two women created a parent education program that provided religious training and Bible study for moms and dads at the same time their kids were in class. Now, instead of waiting in the car or running to the market, parents could learn what their children were learning and discuss it with them that night at the dinner table.

By knowing the members of your team—their hobbies, school background, family, and so forth—you can draw out their hidden talents. These talents might be entirely irrelevant to the person's job but essential to his sense of self. Your chief engineer could be a weekend photographer; the sales manager might be a former track star. Every member of your team has a life outside work, and when you know about it, you can find ways to use their civilian interests in a work context—especially community outreach and charitable fund-raising.

When people give the best part of themselves, they forge a more heartfelt relationship with the company.

It's your job, as manager, to find ways for your employees to do this. You may get turned down the first time you ask the engineer to take photos at the Christmas party, but the fact that you're making the effort will leave an impression. It shows that you know him, you've been listening, and you value his skills. It proves that you see him as more than an engineer. Even if he says, "This isn't the right time for me," he'll be pleased that you asked. When he finally brings his camera to the party, he'll have moved one step closer to the heartfelt commitment that makes a team coalesce.

The detailed description of the construction of the Tent of Meeting makes it clear that Moses put to use every type of gift and every skill the Israelites had to offer. The project was a turning point for the Children of Israel: it was the first time Moses asked them to give to the sanctuary, not simply receive. The act of giving is what seals a relationship, but most people are too shy to give without being asked. Draw them out and they may deliver, as the Israelites did, "more than enough for all the tasks to be done."

24
Find the Willing Minority

"*WHAT SHALL I DO WITH THESE PEOPLE?*"

What manager hasn't looked toward heaven and asked this question? Moses did, and with good reason. The Israelites complained and murmured against him; they were ungrateful for the freedom they had and nostalgic for the life of slavery they'd left behind. As ex-slaves, they had no confidence in themselves; they complained incessantly because they were used to being helpless.

If Moses thought freedom would instantly transform these people, he learned otherwise after the Lord parted the Sea of Reeds. Even a miracle of that magnitude didn't convince the Hebrews to steadfastly trust in God or his servant, Moses. A mere three days later, as they traveled into the wilderness and found no water, they "grumbled against Moses, saying, 'What shall we drink?'" Soon afterward they lamented, "If only we had died by the hand of the Lord in the land of Egypt, when we sat by the fleshpots, when we ate our fill of bread!" Two years later they were still complaining. "If only we had meat to eat! We remember the fish that we used to eat freely in Egypt, the cucumbers, the melons, the leeks." Moses by then knew the tremendous task that lay before him. Among this frightened, helpless flock he must find the few souls hardy enough to conquer Canaan.

When God directed Moses to send twelve spies to Canaan to scout the territory, he provided a character test for Moses' top men. Ten of the spies reported that Canaan did indeed "flow with milk and honey" but that the men who lived there were indomitable. "We looked like grasshoppers to ourselves, and so we must have looked to them." Only two men, Caleb and Joshua, believed the Children of Israel could triumph. "We shall surely overcome it," they said. Moses had found the key: a willing minority who believed in the mission and would help him achieve his goal. Tomorrow's leaders are often found in today's willing minority. Thirty-eight years later, Caleb and Joshua led the Hebrews into Canaan.

In every business, the majority will usually want to take the path of least resistance. There will always be complainers, people who prefer to see the glass half empty. It's a manager's job to motivate these employees, but no manager need do it alone. One of your first goals should be to find the willing minority and use their enthusiasm to help you inspire the others.

The willing minority are people who prove their dedication by actions, not just words. You'll need to discover the men and women who perform when you're not looking, as opposed to those who just "yes" you in meetings. The place to find these employees is in the trenches, when things get tense.

Customer service is the front line of the trenches. The chief engineer at my Image Movement Technology had a telling run-in with the customer service department of a motor manufacturer. When our product, a moving signage system, was in the research and development phase, the motor that drove it inexplicably kept shutting off. Investors from New York were due within weeks, and the engineer was at the end of his rope. He placed call after call to the motor company and talked to a long series of "grasshoppers"—service reps and engineers who told him that the manual must be wrong; there was nothing they could do; the product had some kinks; he'd better try to fix it himself.

Finally he contacted the president of the company. The next day a VP of engineering made the two-hour drive to our lab to personally apologize, roll up his sleeves, and fix the motor. This man renewed our faith in the company and convinced us to keep using their product. The president himself couldn't respond to each and every call of distress, but he did have someone on hand who could say, as Caleb did, "We shall overcome it." While it may be impossible to staff your entire company with Calebs, it's vital to identify at least a few of them.

If you're new to a company, do all you can to find the willing minority. Look for "possibility thinkers" who can envision solutions and new approaches. Don't wait until a crisis strikes; do some investigation. Ask your employees to tell you about past crises and how they were resolved. Make sure you get the names of the people who saved the day. Look over the files of customer complaints, compliments, and suggestions, and pay attention to those employees who receive consistently good marks from sources outside the company.

When you've found your willing minority, nurture them. Enlist them as your allies and hold them up as examples to the rest of the staff. When someone says, "I can't do more than I'm already doing so don't have such high expectations of me," stand with your Caleb and Joshua and reply, "Let's raise the bar, and together we can all jump to the next level."

25
Seek Help from
Within the Family

PEOPLE OF FAITH KNOW THAT THE OLD PROVERB "GOD will provide" is filled with a lot of truth. Sometimes what God provides is not what we think we need, but when that happens, the challenge is to look more closely.

At the burning bush, God already knew Moses would be reluctant to lead the Israelites. "I have never been a man of words," Moses pleaded, in an effort to wriggle out of the assignment. "There is your brother Aaron," countered the Lord. "Even now he is setting out to meet you, and he will be happy to see you." Aaron, God assured Moses, spoke readily. "[I will] tell both of you what to do—and he shall speak for you to the people. Thus he shall serve as your spokesman, with you playing the role of God to him." Sure enough, God's arrangement worked. Throughout the Exodus and the journey that followed, Aaron and Moses worked together to lead the new nation.

In business, as in other areas of life, we tend to look for expertise outside our own house. We seek the fad of the month, the technique of the week. In truth, the best advice often comes from those who are already part of the family. God did not provide Moses with an outside expert or some pricey consultant from Pharaoh's court, but with his own brother. Looking closely, we can understand the wisdom of His choice.

Aaron knew Moses' history. He knew the scope of Moses' mission and that his most difficult task would not be to confront Pharaoh but to persuade the Children of Israel to follow him. Moses didn't have to teach Aaron to be a team player; as a family member, Aaron was already on the team. In coming to meet Moses in the Midianite desert, Aaron showed that he understood where the greatest challenge would take place. The transformation of the Israelites from tribe to nation would occur here, in this harsh wilderness, not in a laboratory with a set of hypothetical assumptions. Aaron knew the turf.

Like Aaron, the people with whom we work every day know the turf. They're eager to share their knowledge and offer suggestions, if only we're willing to listen. Their observations, born of personal experience, are often much more insightful and practical than those of an outsider. Yet looking to the corporate family for advice is so unusual that when it does occur it generates headlines. "Worker Bees Take 'Bold Steps' on County Contracting," crowed an article in the *Los Angeles Times* in the fall of 1998. Business writer Vicki Torres had heard about a report aimed at making Los Angeles County's vast bureaucracy more accessible to small businesses that want to sell it goods and services. "Here's a little tidbit about it that makes the report unique," writes Torres. "It came from the grunts...contracting and purchasing agents who day in and day out saw what was happening and thought there must be a better way."

The biggest problem, in the eyes of the agents, was that mammoth Los Angeles County had no standardized system for handing out its contracts. Every office worked differently. A small group of agents, who had met at a vendor fair and swapped war stories, decided to contact other agents and form the Los Angeles County Contracting and Purchasing Council. The council would review the county's procedures and offer suggestions for streamlining them.

From the beginning, the council ran into opposition from supervisors higher up the food chain. Who had given them permission to form a council? Who were they to review the county's procedures? According to council member Richard Espinosa, "We were just operating on the simple premise that this is the right thing to do. Somebody's got to do it; why not us?"

Several years later the council's report, entitled "Bold Steps Forward," was complete. At first it received not accolades from the big shots, but indifference. Council members didn't give up, however—they formed a small-business advisory board and enlisted the aid of Supervisor Don Knabe, who had made contracting reform one of his campaign issues. At last their report was taken seriously, and in October 1997—five years after the council first met—the county formed an Office of Small Business. Here, at last, was a central location where all county contracts would be posted. The Office of Small Business also maintains a Web site with contract information and is continuing the council's efforts to standardize procedures and make the county more user-friendly to small business.

In all, thirty-five county workers contributed to the council's report. "I think our report could stand up to the reports the county spends thousands of dollars for consultants to do," asserts Espinosa. "We did this on our own time with no charge to the county."

Your business is rich with "human resources" who have a personal stake in its success and an intimate understanding of its operations. In times of crisis, use these resources—look closely at those whom God has already provided before turning to outsiders.

26
Stay Focused on the Big Picture

MOSES HAD PLENTY OF DISTRACTIONS—WATER AND FOOD shortages, complaining compatriots, truculent neighbors, constant requests for advice—not to mention a very demanding boss. He also had a wife and children, although we hear surprisingly little about them. During forty years in the wilderness, it would have been easy to get caught up in the daily tasks of desert survival. Yet with all the distractions and aggravations that surrounded him, Moses never lost sight of the ultimate goal: to bring his people into the Promised Land, having taught them the lessons of ethical monotheism.

Many times, Moses became discouraged. The Bible is full of instances when he turns away from the clamoring tribe and asks for God's guidance. After communing with the Lord, Moses returns to the Israelites re-energized and with a clearer sense of purpose. His story shows us that in order to stay focused, leaders must periodically retreat from the crowd and consult their inner spiritual compass.

Stephen Covey, the renowned author and consultant, believes that one reason it's difficult for today's business people to stay focused is that we waste our energy on "urgent/unimportant" events. We do this, he says, because anything that is urgent tends to *seem* important. The phone ringing, the staff member poking her head in the door, E-mail, pagers, the faxes rolling out of the machine—all of these create a sense of urgency, no matter how unimportant their content may be.

It's essential that we carve out time for reflection amid all these distractions. If we don't take time to refocus on our purpose, we may lose sight of it altogether. The question is: Where do you draw the line? When do you respond to the demands on your time, and when do you hold back? Moses himself struggled to balance accessibility with distance. When he spent too much time in the Tent of Meeting, he was criticized for being remote. When he devoted too much energy to minor affairs, he was accused of micromanaging. Eventually, he seemed to get a feel for when he was needed. Was God telling him when to intervene, or was Moses simply learning the rhythm of management?

Two elements influenced Moses' decisions to step in or keep his distance. First, he was aware that in order for his people to respect him, he would have to hold himself somewhat apart from the group. While he went to great lengths to present himself as a man, not a god, he didn't attempt to be "just one of the guys." Today, many companies have become extremely informal. Everyone is on a first-name basis, and any staffer can E-mail the CEO. The openness is meant to encourage camaraderie and teamwork, but when communication becomes too casual, respect for the leader and his or her responsibilities can diminish. As a manager, you may need to redraw some of those boundaries to gain more time for yourself.

When Moses did intervene in his people's affairs, it was to set a precedent—for instance, when the daughters of Zelophehad appealed to him for their inheritance. Until then, only males could inherit land and the family name. Zelophehad had died and left no sons, only five daughters. "Let not our father's name be lost to his clan just because he had no son," the women implored. "Give us a holding among our father's kinsmen!" Because the resolution of this issue would be an important display of justice, and because it would set the standard for future generations, "Moses brought their case before the Lord," then announced new laws of inheritance: for the first time in the ancient Near East, where strict laws upheld inheritance by the firstborn son, women were able to inherit.

When you become overwhelmed by urgent/unimportant events, ask yourself two questions: Am I too involved in every issue? Is the issue going to set a precedent or serve as an example? By using these general guidelines, you can regain some of your wasted time.

Once you've staked out some moments for reflection, make the most of them. My own vocation has a built-in mechanism for renewal—as a rabbi, I spend a lot of time reading the Bible, which continually refreshes me and keeps me on track. It works in other professions as well. Many constitutional lawyers I know reread the Constitution; in the same way, managers can reread the mission statement or articles of incorporation of their company. They may describe a place radically different from the one that exists today, but reading them will reacquaint you with the founders' philosophy. The perspective you gain will renew your sense of purpose or help you see how far you have come in a new direction.

In the Jewish tradition we have a holiday, Simchat Torah, that celebrates the completion of the cycle of one full reading of the Torah—the five books of Moses. When we finish, we roll the scroll all the way back to the beginning and start again. By continually reading the Bible, we stay in touch with the original, core ideas we value. For managers, this process is every bit as important. There is an old maxim from "Ethics of the Fathers" that says, "Do not say 'I will study the Scriptures when I have the time,' for you may never have the time." Each day, take a little time to refresh and focus on the big picture.

27
Create a Mechanism
for Repair

Moses is famous not only for being a great leader but also for being a flawed one. No beatific guru, he was a passionate, driven man whose moods swung from anger to nervous hand wringing to selfless compassion. Although some Israelites may have revered Moses, many of them undoubtedly had mixed feelings about their leader, in turns resenting, respecting, fearing, and leaning upon him. There's no question that he made mistakes, both in the eyes of his people and in the eyes of God.

Although Moses led the Israelites to the Promised Land, God forbade him to enter it—punishment for overstepping his bounds years earlier. At Kadesh, when the Israelites were hungry, thirsty, and whining (as usual), God told Moses to stand before a rock and "order the rock to yield its water." Feeling cranky, Moses deviated from the plan. He called the people together and taunted them: "Listen, you rebels, shall we get water for you out of this rock?" Then he struck the rock twice, and out poured water.

God was not pleased. He had said to *order* the rock, not *strike* it. God, not Moses, set the terms for miracles. The penalty was that Moses would never enter the Promised Land. A lot of people think this punishment is like being executed for a parking ticket, but the point is that a perfect, flawless role model doesn't exist. It doesn't exist in a president or in corporate CEOs—it doesn't exist in the human condition. Too often, people don't accept the fact that they are dealing with other human beings who are occasionally going to make mistakes. Since (as the law of entropy instructs) breakdowns are inevitable, every organization should anticipate them and have in place a mechanism for repair.

Moses, through God, created such a mechanism at Mount Sinai. When he emerged from atop the mountain only to see a wild orgy taking place before the golden calf, "he became enraged; and he hurled the tablets from his hands and shattered them at the foot of the mountain." God was even angrier than Moses—he wanted to obliterate the Israelites on the spot. Only through Moses' intercession were the people spared divine wrath. But by the next day, having rid the group of members who were not "for the Lord," Moses regained his composure. He told the people, "You have been guilty of a great sin. Yet I will now go up to the Lord; perhaps I may win forgiveness for your sin."

The result, according to biblical commentaries, was the first Yom Kippur, or Day of Atonement. In this ritual, God gave the Israelites a mechanism for rupture, for correcting past mistakes and moving forward. To reap the healing benefits of atonement, you must recognize that you did something wrong, accept responsibility for it, apologize directly to the offended party, and commit to correcting the wrong. If you do that—and if the sin wasn't so egregious that no atonement is possible—you can enter the new year with a clear conscience.

Most mistakes are reparable. Even Moses, who smashed the tablets inscribed by God's own hand, was allowed a second chance. Carve two more tablets, said God, and "I will inscribe upon the tablets the words that were on the first tablets, which you shattered." The second set of tablets were indeed carved, and the Children of Israel moved forward.

"The consumer understands you're going to make mistakes," Bob Pittman, president of America Online, told me. He should know—just weeks after he joined the company in 1997, AOL switched from per-minute pricing to a flat $19.95 a month for unlimited Internet access. Users immediately doubled their time on-line, causing now-legendary busy signals and prompting the nickname "America On Hold." Said Pittman of the snafu: "We're only human, and we've got human beings running this product. But when you make a mistake, people want you to be clear with them. They want you to say, 'I know we have a problem. We're sorry for our part in it. Here is what we're doing to fix it, and here is when you can expect it to be fixed.' I think if you handle that with respect for the consumer, and are truly apologetic, and are working as fast and as hard as you can, they will cut you a break. And I think where you get in trouble is when you start trying to hide things."

America Online did eventually regain its balance and restore consumer confidence. It now boasts more than fifteen million subscribers and owns CompuServe, which has another two million. To maintain customer loyalty, Pittman told me he plans to keep his ears open. "If we listen hard, listen aggressively, listen all the time, we'll stay abreast of what our members need." Being open with your customers even when you make a mistake, and paying close attention to them when times are flush, is good advice for any manager.

Many businesses have had to deal with mistakes, large and small. The smart ones tackle them head-on: They acknowledge their error, accept responsibility, and correct the damage. Then, having regained the public's trust, they can carry on.

28
Trust That Your Creation Will Survive

ACCORDING TO THE ANCIENT SAGES, THE NAME MIRIAM means "bitterness" and Aaron means "Woe unto this pregnancy." What sorrowful names these are—and how vividly they reveal the anguish Moses' parents felt about their children's future. But the worst was yet to come: while Miriam and Aaron were still young, Pharaoh decreed that "every boy that is born you shall throw into the Nile," giving the Egyptians carte blanche to slaughter Hebrew infants. In despair, Moses' mother and father divorced, so that they might never give birth to a son only to watch him be drowned.

According to legend, six-year-old Miriam objected, accusing her parents of being worse than Pharaoh. His decree only prevented boys from living, she argued, but her parents' decision to separate prevented the birth of girls as well. She convinced her parents to remarry, and from this remarriage Moses was born. Without Moses, the liberation, the giving of God's law, and the journey to the Promised Land might never have happened. If Miriam had not urged her parents to throw off their discouragement and open up to the *possibility* of a positive outcome, the world we live in might be a very different place.

How many worthy ideas have been abandoned because people were afraid that once their creation was born, it would never survive? Nearly always, there are "rules" and "evidence" to support the fear that creating a new entity would be a hopeless endeavor. Yet somehow new products, services, and companies do flourish. Behind every one of them is an individual who had to swallow back fear and launch an idea into the marketplace—all the while praying it could somehow survive.

Before Moses could be born, his parents had to believe there was a chance their son might live to adulthood. Similarly, in order to achieve your goals, you must believe there's a good possibility you'll succeed, regardless of conventional wisdom. Talk to any ten visionaries about how they got started, and you'll keep hearing the same story: "People thought I was nuts, but I did it anyway."

Klaus Obermeyer is one such visionary. Obermeyer was born in Germany in 1919 and started skiing at age three on a pair of wooden skis he made from a citrus crate. He had studied to be an aeronautical engineer, but in 1946 he moved to the United States, landing eventually in Aspen, where he taught skiing. There was just one glitch: People were too cold to ski. No one had designed clothing that could keep folks warm on a chairlift, because at that point Aspen had the world's *only* chairlift.

"It was a very cold ride of fifteen minutes, plus another twelve minutes to a warming hut, then twelve more minutes to the top of the mountain," Obermeyer recalled. "I got paid ten dollars per student, but only if they stayed in the class. I kept losing students because they were too cold to ski."

One day, in desperation, he took a down comforter his mother had made, cut it into pieces, and fashioned it into a parka. He wore it to keep himself warm, but a student immediately offered to buy it off his back for $300. That was a lot of money, especially in 1947.

"One of my friends in Germany was a bedding manufacturer," Obermeyer said. "I went there and said to him, 'I want you to take some of this bedding and make a parka.' He told me I was crazy, but I pressured him, and he finally made me seventy-five parkas." They sold like hotcakes, and Obermeyer went on to found Sport Obermeyer and pioneer many other items that are now standard ski wear, including dual construction ski boots, high altitude suntan lotion, mirrored ski sunglasses, and ski jeans.

His company, now in business fifty years, is the only major winter clothing company located in a mountain community. Obermeyer rides the chairlift nearly every day during the winter to talk with skiers and learn what they *don't* like about the experience, so his Sport Obermeyer can develop a product to remedy the situation.

"Any problem is an opportunity disguised," he told me. "We have the choice to be positive or negative, and I have always chosen to be positive."

A few months after my conversation with Klaus Obermeyer, I came across an article I had clipped from *Investor's Business Daily.* The paper had published its "10 Secrets to Success," culled from years of "analyzing leaders and successful people in all walks of life." At the top of the list was, "How you think is everything: Always be positive. Think success, not failure. Beware of a negative environment."

Across the board, people with new ideas are scoffed at or treated with benign indifference, and across the board they forge ahead anyway with a positive attitude. Bob Pittman, current president of America Online, had one of those ideas when he founded MTV: "It seemed perfectly logical to me. We're adding one more dimension to music—a video radio station. But most people said, 'It won't work. Music is meant to be heard, not seen.' Fortunately, they were wrong."

Edwin Land, who founded Polaroid Corporation after inventing Polaroid glass and who later went on to create the instant camera, delighted in alarming his stockholders with seemingly impossible product ideas. "I like to get into situations in which no one believes me," he said. Their disbelief compelled Land to make good on his promises. "Don't do anything that someone else can do," he advised. "Don't undertake a project unless it is manifestly important and nearly impossible"—the better to corner the market for yourself.

In these cases and countless more, men and women persisted through many setbacks and apparent failures. Moses himself is best known for persevering forty years in the wilderness, sustained by his belief. Having a good idea is only the first step on the thousand-mile journey; believing in the idea is what will get you to the Promised Land.

29
Create Team-Building Rituals

WHEN GOD SPOKE TO MOSES, IT WAS USUALLY TO LAY down the law or to give precise directions for some sort of ritual. Few events were left to chance. Listen to His instructions for calling together the troops: "Make for yourself two silver trumpets...they shall be yours for the summoning of the assembly, and to cause the camps to journey. When they sound a long blast with them, the entire assembly shall assemble to you, to the entrance of the Tent of Meeting. If they sound a long blast with one, the leaders shall assemble to you, the heads of Israel's thousands....

"When you go to wage war in your Land against an enemy who oppresses you, you shall sound short blasts of the trumpets, and you shall be recalled before your God, and you shall be saved from your foes.

"On a day of your gladness and on your festivals, and on your new moons, you shall sound the trumpets...and they shall be a remembrance for you before your God."

Why are there so many rituals in the Bible? Because if people had just made up the practices as they went along, they would have missed countless opportunities for what today we call team building. From the simplest to the most complex, rituals are a way for men and women to demonstrate key values and affirm their sense of belonging to a group.

Moses used rituals to help the Children of Israel transform themselves from a sorry band of ex-slaves into a cohesive nation. As a manager, you can choose rituals that will reinforce your organization's values and encourage a sense of belonging among your staff. Your rituals might acknowledge individual achievement, as in making someone "employee of the month" or awarding a top performer a prized parking space. Rituals can help clarify a group's values and generate esprit de corps.

Sapient Corporation uses rituals to help its teams achieve extraordinary success. The company offers a variety of high-tech services, including software and systems integration, custom software development, and production support. Since its founding in 1991, Sapient has nearly doubled its revenues each year to reach 1997 annual revenues of over $90 million—without venture capital or material debt. Equally impressive is Sapient's success in employee satisfaction. The company has a ninety percent acceptance rate for people to whom it offers jobs and the lowest turnover rate in the industry.

Most of Sapient's business involves putting together teams to work on-site at their client's location and stay there until a solution is in place. When a project is complete, the team is disbanded and the members dispatched to other clients to become part of new teams. Jon Frey, a director at Sapient who has managed a wide variety of team projects, offers some insights as to how the company creates and recreates teams so effectively.

"Before projects start," he says, "We have 'team weeks,' which are designed to build a strong team. During that week we help team members understand the abilities of each person and build a cohesive group." During team week, the team generates its own unique rituals. "Each team comes up with its own cheer," says Frey. "Coming up with a cheer builds unity and makes them feel empowered. Then, when we are on-site with the client, we end every meeting with the team cheer."

Another productivity builder that Sapient uses is standing meetings—and they do mean standing. The team meets every morning, and everyone stands throughout the meeting. "With everyone standing up, you tend to get done a lot quicker," notes Frey.

Team meetings also provide a venue for acknowledging the contributions of team members. Recalls Frey, "On one project, we also instituted 'Bud Awards.' At each team meeting, someone would nominate a member for the Bud Award. If the team member had gone beyond the call of duty in meeting the client's needs, or had a breakthrough on a particularly difficult project, he might be nominated. When we reached specific project milestones we had a Bud party. Everyone would come to my house. I would put a yellow sticky note on their can of beer that said what they had gotten the award for." The team didn't do their work to get the beer—they felt empowered and excited about doing their job because they understood that their client and their teammates counted on them to deliver. But the cheers, the meetings, and the milestone parties helped maintain the team spirit.

To one observer, Sapient's methods clearly achieved the desired results. Steve Kroll, vice president of marketing for Answer Financial, Inc., witnessed a Sapient group in action as it developed a high-level Internet server for his company. "There was an underlying sense of team spirit," he recalls. "It was not a question of how they felt about the task; it was that they couldn't let the team down. Their attitude was, 'I'm never going to make a mistake because it would reflect poorly on my teammates.' That was what made them special in my mind."

Whatever rituals you choose to institute, be sure to link them to your core values. Moses' rituals reflected his belief in God and in the importance of an ethical set of common rules. You're not trying to recreate the Bible, and your task is a lot simpler, but your rituals will still give form to your beliefs. Use rituals to demonstrate to your employees what you consider to be important and to give them a tangible way of knowing they belong.

30
Resolve Conflicts Quickly and Objectively

BOARDROOM COUPS ARE NOTHING NEW. AS IF MOSES didn't have enough problems dealing with Pharaoh, parting the Sea of Reeds, and being the ombudsman between a cantankerous tribe of ex-slaves and a some-times testy God, he also had to respond to an open rebellion. The leader of the insurrection was a man named Korach.

Korach had little trouble gathering a group of mal-contents to his cause. Together with 250 Israelites, "they combined against Moses and Aaron and said to them, 'You have gone too far! For all the community are holy, all of them, and the Lord is in their midst. Why then do you raise yourselves above the Lord's congregation?'"

This must have been a bitter moment indeed for Moses, considering that he had never wanted the mission in the first place and had by now endured years of the Israelites' grousing. His response was swift and decisive: "He spoke to Korach and all his company saying, 'Come morning, the Lord will make himself known who He is and who is holy, and will grant access to Himself; He will grant access to the one He has chosen. Do this: You, Korach, and all your band, take fire pans and tomorrow put fire in them and lay incense on them before the Lord. Then the man whom the Lord chooses, he shall be the holy one.'"

The next morning, we can imagine the scene: Moses and Aaron with their pan of incense and 250 rebels standing by with theirs. Moses says, "'By this you shall know that it was the Lord who sent me to do all these things; that they are not of my own devising: if these men die as all men do, if their lot be the common fate of all mankind, it was not the Lord who sent me. But if the Lord brings about something unheard-of, so that the ground opens up its mouth and swallows them up with all that belongs to them, and they go down alive into Sheol, you shall know that these men have spurned the Lord.' Scarcely had he finished speaking all these words when the ground under them burst asunder, and the earth opened its mouth and swallowed them up with their households."

Those who sided with Korach disappeared forever into a pit in the ground, and those who stood with Moses lived. No doubt there are times when you've wished you could resolve your own power struggles so conclusively! Alas, the days of open miracles are over, but we can still find lessons in conflict resolution from the way Moses responded to Korach.

His first move was to stall for time by telling everyone to return the next morning and see how the conflict would be resolved. Buying time is often an excellent first step in diffusing a charged situation. However, he didn't postpone resolution for long, only until the next day. This ensured that Korach would not be able to garner any more support than he already had.

Moses' second strategy was to appeal to an outside party to judge the relative merits of their positions. He didn't let himself get dragged into the conflict. Instead, he immediately realized that God should resolve the matter. He had clear criteria for interpreting God's decision: If Korach either lived on or died a normal death, Moses would step down as God's spokesman. But if Korach and his allies died in a completely novel way, this would prove that God had singled out Moses as their leader.

This plan of action is still extremely effective. When a power struggle erupts, it makes sense to first call for a brief cooling-off period. If things haven't calmed down after that period, call in a third party—a consultant, a mediator, or an arbitrator. "Let God decide between us," said Moses, but your mediator doesn't need to be that omnipotent. He or she just needs to understand the basic issues and have experience in conflict resolution.

Contemporary business leaders are increasingly finding that outside arbitration is preferable to an extended court battle. Diana Peterson-More, a professional mediator and president of the Organizational Effectiveness Group in Pasadena, California, believes that appealing to the participants' shared goals is a powerful way to resolve conflict. Peterson-More recalled a time she was asked to settle a dispute between the production and postproduction staffs of a motion picture. The studio asked her to help smooth out a familiar conflict in that industry: If the production crew goes over budget, they take money from postproduction; then, when the postproduction crew runs out of money, *they* get blamed for going over budget. On this particular film, the heads of each division were fuming. "I got them together and focused on the fact that their ultimate goals were the same. They both wanted financial and professional success. When people can agree on the business objectives, they can start to see that even though the system is designed to pit them against each other, they have the choice to make it work. These individuals agreed to talk openly about their real constraints and budgets and to work together toward their shared goals."

This is the sort of resolution that can only occur with the help of a third party. Sometimes issues that have dragged on for months can be decided in an afternoon once an objective voice enters the discussion. When people take their attention off the personalities and focus on solving their shared problem, many tensions dissipate. Rafael Lapin, a mediator in San Jose, California, recalls a case where two people who had owned a beauty salon franchise decided to dissolve their partnership. The problem was that they couldn't distribute the funds because they couldn't agree on who had put the most effort into the business and generated more profits. Finally, they called Lapin. "We've been discussing this for six months," they told him, "so we thought we should have someone else make the decision." Two hours later, they walked out with an agreement that satisfied them both.

Arbitration was Moses' tool for dealing with Korach quickly. It is just as valuable a strategy today. Don't get dragged down into the muck of a conflict;

get it resolved. That's what your superiors are going to be looking for. They don't want to know about the drama, and they don't want to hear the details. They just want you to handle it. If you can tell them, "I had a cooling-off period, then I called in an outside arbitrator and we resolved it," you'll be following in the footsteps of a master.

31
Watch for Burning Bushes

THE EVENT THAT CATAPULTED MOSES FROM ANONYMOUS shepherd to religious leader began as an odd quirk of nature. As he was out tending his father-in-law's flock, "he gazed, and there was a bush all aflame, yet the bush was not consumed. Moses said, 'I must turn aside to look at this marvelous sight; why doesn't the bush burn up?' When the Lord saw that he had turned aside to look, God called to him out of the bush: 'Moses! Moses!'"

If Moses had not noticed something that was off the beaten path and turned aside to see what it was, he might have missed his shot at revelation. A bush that burned and was not consumed was certainly an unlikely sight, but Moses could have walked right past it. He didn't. He turned off his path and went to learn more about it. He was curious rather than fearful; he noticed his surroundings as opposed to sleepwalking through them. His experience at the burning bush serves as a model for entrepreneurs and managers of all stripes.

"Management must watch for low-probability, high-impact events," observes Moshe Rubenstein, a professor at UCLA's Anderson Graduate School of Management and, with Iris Firstenberg, coauthor of *The Minding Organization*. "Moses paid attention to events that had nothing to do with his leadership (or his shepherding), something far afield. He saw something that wasn't consumed. This was something highly unlikely, but if you discovered a material that is not consumed, you could make a fortune.... Intel and Microsoft will make acquisitions of many burning bushes which are low in probability of success but which, if they do materialize, will create a revolution in areas that may not exist yet."

As we walk down our own paths, we all encounter "burning bushes"—anomalous events, odd coincidences, quirky insights for new uses of old products. But how many of us turn off our path, as Moses did, to see whether a life-changing revelation awaits us? Eric Gould, president of batna.com, a mediation training firm, says, "It's vital to question inconsistencies. Even if we *see* that the burning bush is different, we might not ask *why* it is different. But the why is important. We need to ask ourselves what each event is trying to communicate."

One lesson the burning bush incident teaches is that we need to be willing to look around and explore opportunities that other people overlook. As Gould points out, many successful products have been launched by people who saw new possibilities in things that others considered worthless. "Fake logs are just wood chips," he says. "Someone went out and collected these scraps from lumber mills. They threw in lighter fluid and packed it all together and wrapped it up." And the world had a new product.

Seeing gold where others see garbage may sound farfetched, but it happens regularly. Seattle's Jon Rowley saw not gold but copper—Copper River king salmon. In 1982, Rowley became aware that the salmon, a highly flavorful variety that originates in Alaska's Copper River, were getting caught in the holds of fishing boats. There the fish soaked in bilge water, its fine flavor and value disintegrating. The salmon were eventually sold to canneries at a cut-rate price.

Jon Rowley began his own save-the-salmon campaign. "I persuaded my fishing buddies that if they could handle the fish properly, I could market it for them as premium fresh fish and get them a better price," he told the *Seattle Times.* The idea worked. Row-ley is now credited with starting the Copper River salmon phenomenon, a near frenzied demand for the fish during the one month a year it is available, from mid-May until mid-June. How great is the appetite for the salmon? One Seattle restaurant, Ray's Boathouse, sells three tons of it in that single month.

It's very easy to plow from one task to another, thinking that we know what our job is and where we're going. In fact, our real opportunity might be just out-side our standard field of vision, in a pile of scrap wood or the hold of a fishing boat. Our path to great-ness might not lie at the end of our current path at all, but off a side road, at our burning bush.

32
Don't Be Blinded
by Your Own Power

AFTER GOD APPEARED TO MOSES IN THE BURNING BUSH, after He dispensed with Moses' objections and laid out His plan to free the slaves, He threw in something else almost as an afterthought: "I, however, will stiffen [Pharaoh's] heart so that he will not let the people go." This sentence has perplexed many readers. If God was all-powerful and wanted the Israelites to escape Egypt, why didn't he *soften* Pharaoh's heart?

Part of the answer has to do with the power struggle between God and Pharaoh. "I will harden Pharaoh's heart, that I may multiply My signs and marvels," says the Lord. The more stubborn the pharaoh, the more opportunities God will have to prove to both the

Egyptians and the Israelites that He is the mightier of the two. Pharaoh, living the life of a king, hardly felt the plagues on more than a personal ego level. Even the Egyptian people were inclined to see only a contest of kings, not the glory of God.

"[Tell] your sons' sons how I made a mockery of the Egyptians and how I displayed My signs among them," God instructs Moses. The ten plagues are meant to settle the power dispute forever and ensure that the Israelites will "have no other Gods besides Me." But another lesson is also embedded in the Lord's decision to harden Pharaoh's heart. It has to do with the heavy price Pharaoh paid for his arrogance and isolation.

Ancient Egypt was one of history's most rigid hierarchies. Pharaoh was no mere ruler but a god to his people; he owned not only the Israelites but every Egyptian man, woman, and child. Egypt truly was a "house of bondage" for every citizen who lived there. So great was Pharaoh's power that despite Egypt's sophistication in other areas—architecture, language, art, commerce—it never had a code of law. Pharaoh was the law.

When Moses first told Pharaoh of the Lord's instruction to "let My people go," Pharaoh's response was, "Who is the Lord that I should heed him and let

Israel go? I do not know the Lord, nor will I let Israel go." His arrogance prevented him from taking Moses seriously, not only on that first day, but year after year, plague after plague. Egypt had already suffered a befouled Nile river, frogs, lice, insects, hail storms, and cattle disease when God told Moses to once again go to Pharaoh, and this time warn him that a plague of locusts would be next. After Moses delivered the message, Pharaoh's own courtiers dared to approach. They must have been desperate men, cowering as they pleaded with their god-king: "How long shall this one [Moses] be a snare to us? Let the men go to worship the Lord their God! Are you not yet aware that Egypt is lost?"

Therein lies the lesson. A leader that arrogant, that tied to the old ways, that cut off from the events around him, will not be aware that the nation is lost. A leader who is all-powerful will often bring down his own society. What Moses learned from Pharaoh, and what all successful managers must bear in mind, is that the more isolated and arrogant a leader becomes, the less able he is to see the big picture clearly and act rationally.

Recent history is filled with examples of people and industries so arrogant that they become blind to their surroundings. Among the most notorious are the big three U.S. auto manufacturers who, in the 1970s and 1980s, entirely misjudged the appeal of well-designed, gas-thrifty Japanese cars to the American public. Toyota and Nissan established a beachhead and grabbed a market share while the U.S. automakers slumbered.

Individuals are just as vulnerable when they allow their wealth or power to isolate them. During George Bush's 1992 election campaign, he paid a visit to the National Grocers Association convention. Arriving at a mock checkout stand, Bush marveled at the bar-code reader. As described in the *New York Times* the following day, "[a] look of wonder flickered across his face" as he scanned a quart of milk and watched the price appear on the cash register screen. "Some grocery stores began using electronic scanners as early as 1976," the *Times* reminded its readers. By that night, Americans everywhere knew just how out of touch Mr. Bush was with the lives of ordinary citizens. It badly hurt his credibility.

The typical manager spends much time trying to accrue power and territory and gives little thought to their flip side—arrogance and isolation. Entrepreneurs in particular often resist sharing control of the companies they started from scratch. It's certainly easier to get things done if you don't have to wade through the opinions of others, but to work in isolation is to risk being blindsided by rapidly changing events. Listening to your team—not just issuing orders—is often the only way to get the job done and acquire the information you need to succeed.

Diana Peterson-More, president of the Organizational Effectiveness Group in Pasadena, California, does executive coaching and mediation for corporations nationwide. She points out that people in positions of power often don't get honest feedback from their subordinates, and that this contributes to the power-blindness they sometimes experience. Says Peterson-More, "I recall one case in which I was asked to do a 360-degree evaluation for the head of marketing and merchandising of a major manufacturing corporation. This man was very creative, very strong, and very rude and nasty. Even though people were quitting left, right, and center, and he was terminating people frequently, he never thought it had to do with him. When he got the feedback, he realized the problem was that he was always telling, never asking.

"Unfortunately, by the time the information came in, the situation was too far gone and the company terminated him. The problem is that if a person has been unkind, condescending, and rude long enough, the people around him just don't believe it when he seems to change. When I did a follow-up evaluation, one of his staff members said, 'I just keep waiting for the other shoe to drop.' If he had been made aware earlier, he might have been able to regain the trust of the people around him. As it was, he had caused too much pain for far too long, and the senior management felt he had to go."

No leader is so mighty that he or she can afford to assume the role of Pharaoh. Even Moses, who prevailed over the Egyptian king, is described by the Bible as "a very humble man, more so than any man on earth." Far from placing himself above his comrades, he willingly listened to them and often took their advice. Although he alone spoke face-to-face with God, he was wise enough to listen not just to God, but also to his people.

33
Establish Creative Downtime

W<small>ORKING SEVEN DAYS A WEEK DOESN'T MAKE PEOPLE ANY</small> more productive. In fact, it wears them down. That is why the Sabbath was so important to God—by example and by command, he showed Moses and the Israelites that one day a week, all work must cease so that they may rest and contemplate things of a higher order. The Fourth Commandment says, "Remember the Sabbath day to keep it holy. Six days you shall labor, and do all your work, but the seventh day is a Sabbath of the Lord your God: you shall not do any work—you, or your son or daughter, your male or female slave, or your cattle, or the stranger who is within your settlements." In other words, *everybody* is entitled to a day of rest.

In his outstanding book *Seven Habits of Highly Effective People*, Stephen Covey writes about the habit of "sharpening the saw." The term is based on a story of two men who are competing to see who can cut down more trees within a given time period. One man stops every hour to sharpen his saw. The other looks at him and laughs, saying, "How can you stop sawing? Don't you know our time is limited?" At the end, the man who stopped to sharpen his saw has cut the most trees. Every living being needs cycles of activity and rest.

Our culture has a pernicious tendency to try to fill all free time with some type of activity. If we are not working eighty-hour weeks, we're supposed to be *doing* something to unwind. A billboard for a sports club near my home in Los Angeles shows an attractive young woman dressed in tight gym clothes, wearing big red boxing gloves. The caption is: "You can rest when you're dead." That's a cheery thought—we can all keep punching away until we drop dead. Personally, I like to keep a little more balance in my life.

Balance is what the Sabbath is all about. Six days shall you run around like crazy trying to get all your work and errands done, but one day of the week is set aside to reflect on life and its source. One day a week, we can simply let things be. I know for myself that if my religion did not dictate that I take Saturdays off, I'd be tempted to squeeze in a little work or just a couple of errands every week—and before I knew it, I'd be back on the hamster wheel of perpetual motion. So it is helpful for me to have a faith that requires me to take a day of rest.

A similar dynamic occurs in the workplace. It's easy for employees to ignore coffee breaks and wolf down lunch at their desks if their corporate culture encourages that sort of behavior. Instead, urge your staff to take breaks and reasonable lunch hours. Some managers go even further, fostering a culture in which "creative downtime" is a structured part of each workday. Sport Obermeyer in Aspen, Colorado, is staffed by skiers and snowboarders. Founder Klaus Obermeyer encourages his employees to get out on the slopes or enjoy some other sport every day. "To gain the most enjoyment in life, you must be happy in your job," he says. Obermeyer told me that he himself spends an hour each day at tennis, swimming, or skiing. He models the behavior he wants to see in his employees: an exuberance for life and an appreciation of play as well as work.

Peter Ritchie, a businessman and entrepreneur who is chairman of McDonald's in Australia, speaks passionately about the importance of balance in work-family matters. "Balance in work and life are hugely important. If you don't have this sorted out, you won't be much use to anyone. You won't be doing the right thing by your family and you'll only be pretending that the hours you're putting in at work are good. Don't get me wrong—hard work and effort are essential, but there are other things too. People who don't take time out to reflect on how things are going, who keep running the race without a plan, who put in longer and longer hours, will be unstable because they'll be unbalanced. They'll be doing poor work if they're exhausted."

As a manager, you can help your employees stay balanced by creating a culture in which the value of creative downtime is clear. Don't make people call in sick when they are really suffering from mental and emotional overload. Encourage them to get out of the building and smell the flowers (if there are any) during lunchtime. Most of all, be a model of humanity yourself. Remember the man hacking away at the tree with a dull saw—it's not the act of sawing you're after, it's the quantity of chopped trees. By allowing yourself and your staff periods of time when they are not working at all, you will ultimately generate better results.

Scientific history is full of stories about great discoveries that were made when periods of intense concentration were followed by a time for play and relaxation. Biographies of Albert Einstein describe how he struggled with the theory of relativity, and then finally gave up and went for a walk in the woods with a close friend. As they strolled along and Einstein chatted about his work, he suddenly understood it all. His friend reported that Einstein ran all the way back to his laboratory so he could write down his insight before it escaped him.

God decreed that the Children of Israel should work for six days and rest for one. Perhaps one-to-seven is a good ratio to use when gauging how much time you should allot your staff for regeneration each day. Being busy every minute is not the ultimate goal in life. Creating a rhythm of activity and rest, exertion and rejuvenation, will better enable you to set your goals and achieve them.

34
Let Others Share
Your Burden

MOSES HADN'T JOURNEYED WITH THE ISRAELITES MORE than a few months before the task began to overwhelm him, but like many leaders, he was unaware of the approaching burnout. It took an outsider—his father-in-law, Jethro—to show him the light. Jethro had brought Moses' wife Zipporah and their two sons to join him on the trip to Mount Sinai. The group caught up with Moses at Rephidim, where the Israelites had stopped to camp. The day after they arrived, Jethro witnessed what he instantly recognized as a dangerous scenario: Surrounded by people from dawn till dusk, Moses was patiently settling disputes and counseling individuals on the laws and teachings of God.

"What is this thing that you are doing to the people?" questioned Jethro. "Why do you act alone, while all the people stand about you from morning until evening?...You will surely wear yourself out, and these people as well. For the task is too heavy for you; you cannot do it alone. Now listen to me. I will give you counsel.... You represent the people before God, and enjoin upon them the laws and teachings.... You shall also seek out from among all the people capable men who fear God, trustworthy men who spurn ill-gotten gain. Set them over them as chiefs of thousands, hundreds, fifties, and tens, and let them judge the people at all times. Have them bring every major dispute to you, but let them decide every minor dispute themselves. Make it easier for yourself by letting them share the burden with you. If you do this—and God so commands you—you will be able to bear up; and all the people too will go home unwearied."

As a manager, you can learn three important lessons from this conversation between Moses and Jethro. First, don't even attempt to do it all. Find competent people and give them real responsibilities. Second, if you find yourself struggling to do it all as your organization grows, take a long, hard look at the way your business is structured. Don't fall into the "founder's trap" of micromanaging daily details while neglecting the larger strategic issues. Third, when someone gives you good advice, follow it. If Moses could take advice from his father-in-law, you can probably take advice from anyone.

If you don't delegate, some aspect of your life will surely suffer. Even if your business thrives, your personal relationships will not. It's no coincidence that it was Jethro who insisted that Moses cut back on his work hours—undoubtedly he wanted to make sure his son-in-law wouldn't be too exhausted to spend time with Zipporah and the kids. Eventually even the most driven entrepreneur must face the fact that in order to thrive, you have to delegate.

"Driven" hardly begins to describe Dennis Holt, the founder of Western International Media. In 1969 Holt opened shop in Los Angeles, envisioning a media-buying entity that would pool the resources of small ad agencies to give them the same sort of clout the large agencies had. He hung up his shingle in a small office across the street from the famous Pink's Hot Dog Stand. In 1994 Western—by then the largest independent media-buying operation in the United States—was sold to Interpublic Group of Companies for $50 million. Holt, who agreed to the sale in order to gain access to global markets, stayed on as president and continued to work seven days a week.

The Holt work ethic is most tellingly characterized by a method he employed to keep competitors on their toes. "I used to park my car right in a place where the competitors could see it. So they would say to people, 'I went by his office on a Saturday morning, and he's there. He's always there. God, enough.' Which is psychologically very important—having the competition always off balance." Holt concedes, however, that this level of commitment came at a price: "That's what caused my divorce."

When I asked him about his leadership style, Holt described it as "a curse. I am totally hands-on. I don't delegate. I am not a delegator." But in recent years, he admitted, "I've had to do that." In 1996, Holt took the plunge and delegated big time: He promoted COO Michael Kassan to president and assumed the title chairman and chief executive for himself. Says Holt, "Michael is a great delegator and a very good manager."

Holt's faith in Kassan is palpable. The two share many of the same values, especially a commitment to hard work. Says Kassan, "Everybody in this company, two thousand people strong, knows that there's not anybody willing to work harder than Dennis Holt or Michael Kassan." Both men also view the company as family, and consider loyalty among family members to be paramount.

Toward the end of our conversation, Kassan mentioned that Holt had hired him despite his lack of experience in the field of media buying. "It was intuition that Michael would be right for this job," confirmed Holt. The fact that they shared so many core values no doubt made Holt more comfortable ceding some of his power to Kassan. I noticed, too, that Dennis Holt instinctively understands the benefit of taking advice from others. "I tell people all the time, 'Protect me from me,'" he says.

After I interviewed Holt and Kassan, Dennis sent me a list of his favorite quotations. At the top of the page was:

> Two stonecutters were asked what they were doing. The first said, "I'm cutting this stone into blocks." The second replied, "I'm on a team that's building a cathedral."

Dennis Holt obviously recognizes the importance of teamwork and delegation. But halfway down the page was this quote:

> If you are not the lead dog, the view is always the same.

Can the two viewpoints coexist? They can. Delegating doesn't mean you'll be giving up the alpha dog position. It just means that your burden will be lighter, your focus sharper, your energy stronger. But you have to trust the people to whom you are delegating. Jethro told Moses not to appoint ten brilliant men or ten powerful men, but ten capable, *trustworthy* men. As you search for the individuals who can help share your burden, look not only for those who can do the work but also for those who are trustworthy and share your vision.

35
Maintain Ties with People Who Move On

MOSES WASN'T ABOVE USING FORCE TO KEEP HIS BAND OF followers together during their sojourn in the wilderness. Especially at the beginning, the Lord directed him to take a rigid stand against those who strayed from His law. People who were found working on the Sabbath were stoned, those who worshipped the golden calf were disposed of, and the rebel Korach along with 250 of his followers were swallowed into the earth. When attempting to civilize thousands of panicky ex-slaves, such stern measures were sometimes necessary for survival.

As the Children of Israel gathered by the banks of the Jordan River gearing up to conquer the Promised Land, Moses again encountered a group who desired to break away. The tribes of Reuben and Gad had "abundant livestock." They saw that the land east of the Jordan was perfect for grazing their flocks. So they came to Moses and said, "It would be a favor to us... if this land were given to your servants as a holding; do not move us across the Jordan." Moses replied, "Are your brothers to go to war while you stay here?" In other words, he told them to forget it. Going across the Jordan and conquering Canaan had been the common goal for forty years—they couldn't bow out now.

Then Gad and Reuben proposed a compromise. "We will build here sheepfolds for our flocks and towns for our children. We will hasten as shocktroops in the vanguard of the Israelites until we have established them in their home.... We will not return to our homes until every one of the Israelites is in possession of his portion. But we will not have a share with them in the territory beyond the Jordan, for we have received our share on the east side of the Jordan."

That is, they promised to linger only long enough to secure their flocks and build shelter for their families, and then they would go with the group and help the Israelites attain their goal. After that, they would return to take possession of the grazing lands.

Moses accepted the plan. Unlike earlier instances of defiance, the tribes of Gad and Reuben were not rebelling so much as determining their own destiny. They had been faithful throughout the journey; they deserved to live on the land that could best support them. Moses could have insisted they stay with the group permanently, but it probably wouldn't have worked. Since he couldn't force them to remain with the others, he wisely chose to compromise, using their energy to help secure Canaan and then parting ways amicably.

In any group, be it business or nonprofit, there will be individuals and clusters of people who outgrow the organization. Even if you give them opportunities to carve out their own niche within the company, they'll want to move on. It's not that they're rebelling or rejecting you, it's just that they sense greener pastures on the other side of the river. In some industries, particularly high-tech and communications, there is so much opportunity out there that certain employees are bound to take the entrepreneurial plunge. You can cast them out of your golden circle, or you can make use of their expertise, as Moses did, and maintain strong, potentially profitable ties with them. Who better to serve as a consultant than someone who already knows your staff and product line? Who better to use as a vendor than the person who once bought the same supplies for your company?

Michael Dell, Chairman and CEO of Dell Computer Corporation, touches on this subject in his book *Direct from Dell: Strategies That Revolutionized an Industry.* "Once a reporter asked me which of our competitors represented the biggest threat to Dell," he writes. "I said the biggest threat to Dell wouldn't come from a competitor. It would come from our people. It hasn't been easy, trying to maintain the entrepreneurial spirit that has characterized Dell as our company has grown bigger (in terms of headcount) and more complicated (by way of infrastructure). Nor has it been easy to maintain the energy of a focused team as we've expanded around the world. But my goal has always been to make sure that everyone at Dell feels they are part of something great—something special—perhaps something even greater than themselves."

Most managers would agree with Dell's goals and with his assessment of how difficult those goals are to reach. While Michael Dell does everything he can to promote employee loyalty—offering stock ownership, 401K plans, and so forth—it's interesting to note that much of his book talks about developing relationships with suppliers and customers. He relies as heavily on good relationships with suppliers as he does on his workers. This emphasis on a strong link to outside sources is the wave of the future, and it is here that we gain some insight about maintaining ties with employees who move on.

Dell calls the process "virtual integration," as opposed to the old model of vertical integration. In vertical integration, a company attempts to acquire all the physical assets necessary to produce a product. For instance, a company such as Dell, which sells custom-built computers direct to the consumer, would try to stock all the parts that make up the computers. In contrast, Dell uses virtual integration: "By creating information partnerships with customers and suppliers, Dell has obtained the benefits of tightly coordinated supply chain management that have normally been associated with vertically integrated companies." In other words, Dell orders supplies only as they are needed, rather than warehousing them. To do this, Dell must cultivate seamless relationships with both suppliers and customers.

These relationships are the secret to Dell's success. Likewise, the relationships you maintain with people outside your company—especially those who leave your employ on good terms—are priceless. They can be as valuable an asset as physical commodities.

Sometimes ex-employees can become saviors of the companies they once worked for. Bonnie Watts, now sixty-four, recently bought the Rock Hill Printing &

Finishing Company plant in York, South Carolina—forty-eight years after he started work there as a sixteen-year-old spare hand. Watts dropped out of school to join the same company where both his father and mother had worked until retirement. After twenty-eight years at the plant, he realized that "there could be a niche in the market for a small company with a couple of machines." He founded York Printing & Finishing, which now finishes two to three million yards of fabric per year. When Watts heard that his old plant was going to be closed down, he went into motion. After securing a government-backed loan, he purchased Rock Hill. "We will be hiring former employees, some who are seventy years old and higher," he said.

Moses knew that people who have outgrown the organization can make ideal partners. Before granting Gad and Reuben's request for land, he told them, "Build towns for your children and sheepfolds for your flocks, but do what you have promised." Similarly, if a cluster of bright employees is leaving the company and you can't talk them out of it, give them your blessing. Use their expertise for as long as you can, and forge an alliance with them once they are out on their own. In this way, instead of losing them altogether, you'll fortify the relationships upon which your organization depends.

36
Use Exile to
Reinvent Yourself

EXILE IS A FRIGHTENING WORD. TO BE EXILED IS TO BE CAST out, separated from all that is familiar and comfortable. As the Bible so memorably puts it, an exile is "a stranger in a strange land." Moses felt like a foreigner for many years during his exile in Midian. He even named his firstborn son Gershom, meaning "a stranger there." But despite his uneasiness, it was exile that made Moses a man worthy of God's mission. Exile changed him from an unfocused rebel to a faithful shepherd and eventually to an impassioned leader.

Moses fled Egypt because he had killed an Egyptian taskmaster who was beating a Hebrew slave. This was hardly the first time Moses would have seen such brutality, but it was the first time he did anything about it. A line had been crossed—he could no longer tolerate the injustice of slavery. Yet while Moses was willing to defend one slave, he was by no means ready to lead six-hundred thousand of them in a revolt against the king. Perhaps, then, slaying the taskmaster was an act of self-sabotage. Maybe he knew he'd be forced to flee Egypt, and once in exile, he could realize his true calling. Carl Jung once said, "When an inner situation is not made conscious, it appears outside as fate."

Of course, Moses could have left Egypt on his own, without killing anyone. He could have exiled himself. But he didn't—none of us do. We don't exile ourselves because we don't want to leave the comfortable lives we've created. Even Moses, horrified as he was at the Egyptians' cruelty, wasn't able to wrench himself away from that culture voluntarily. He had to be pushed out. Moses faced a struggle we all face: whether to heed an inner voice that's urging us to take on a challenge, or stay in the comfort of known surroundings.

We'll never know if Moses heard an inner voice at the moment he struck the taskmaster, but he clearly was not prepared to make the shift from prince to liberator in a single act. He needed time to think, grow, gain new skills, and solidify his ideas. That kind of reinvention could take place only when he had left behind all the comforts of home and thrown himself into new territory. In other words, it could only happen in exile.

During his exile in Midian, Moses grew to manhood. He became a husband and father, and he created a place for himself in a new community. Having been raised in the luxury of Pharaoh's court, Moses now learned to fend for himself in the desert. Because of the survival skills he learned during his exile, he was able to guide the Hebrew slaves through the wilderness years later. In Midian, Moses became a shepherd, which ultimately was his mission in life. The shepherd's staff became a symbol of his leadership and of God's power. Exile created Moses, the leader.

One modern equivalent of exile is termination—another word that fills us with dread. To be cast out of your job, separated from the comfort of a paycheck, and divorced from your title and the respect that goes with it can feel like a catastrophe. But, as was the case with Moses, exile can force you to reach levels you otherwise would never attempt.

At one point in my life, I was not renewed at the temple I had led for nearly eight years. It was also a time of great crisis for me and my family: My late wife had an advancing cancer and our son was only six years old. With my wife's inspiring help, I determined to create a new temple that would blend religion and the arts, a temple that I would both lead and administer. Seven years later, my temple has two thousand congregants. A dream born out of adversity has been realized.

The strangeness of exile can be terrifying at first. It's true that some people who lose their jobs or undergo other types of exile—an illness or accident, for instance—become depressed and never fully recover. Most, however, surprise themselves with their resiliency. A story is told concerning the opening of a pharaoh's tomb. Among the treasures, archaeologists found food that had been intended for the pharaoh's journey to the next world. As an experiment, they took one barley seed and dropped it into a jar of water. Miraculously, it sprouted. Imagine a seed thousands of years old springing to life! Deep within each of us is the seed of renewal, often discovered only when we confront the fears of change, rejection, and exile. If you can believe that the experience of exile will push you to greater heights, that belief will help you get through the initial shock to the revelations that adversity can bring.

Tom Shapiro is the founder of Academy Tent and Canvas, one of the largest tent and party rental companies in the United States. Since 1981, Academy has provided tenting for the Super Bowl, the Kentucky Derby, the Academy Awards, the Atlanta and Los Angeles Olympics, and many other high-visibility events. Tom didn't start out in the tenting business. He was set to inherit the family company, a ladies' coat and suit manufacturer. Surprisingly, his father warned him away from the job. "He didn't think it was a very good business to go into. In fact, he said it was like being a buggy whip manufacturer—there just weren't very many buggies around anymore." Shapiro joined the firm anyway, but his father proved to be right. Slowly, the business died.

"I had the responsibility of closing the company down. It was truly the most painful business experience of my life. We had employees who had been with my grandfather and my father, and we had to terminate them." After liquidating the stock and shutting the doors on the fifty-five-year-old concern, Shapiro went home and waited. "The reward for being liquidated was that no one even called to offer me a job! I then went through the three most agonizing months of my career. I was out of work and didn't know what I was going to do or how I was going to earn a living. It was quite an awakening for me to go from a family business where everything was handed to you on a platter, to nothing." But as painful as those months were, Shapiro is grateful for them. "That became a motivational driving force for me, because I remember what that was like, and I'll never go back."

Eventually Shapiro did find work with a firm that manufactured canvas tents and awnings. The owner paid a good salary, but, more important, he promised Shapiro that he would one day sell him the company. "He said he wanted me to learn the business from the ground up, and I did. I was there very long hours. I viewed it as a can't-lose situation—either he'd sell me his business or I'd learn an industry." Three and a half years later, Shapiro approached the owner to ask for a written commitment about selling the company. The owner agreed, but a few weeks later Shapiro got a call from the man's lawyer: He was reneging on his promise. There would be no sale.

This was the second "exile" Tom Shapiro experienced in his business life. "It was another low point that, looking back, was really a high point. That's one of the lessons you learn: You really can't judge something at first, because what may seem like a negative situation can actually be a blessing."

Shapiro teamed up with a partner and started Academy Tent. From this business he went on to found a second company and buy a third. The fact that his former boss was now a competitor lit a fuse under Shapiro. "When he reneged and we had to start up our own company, I had more zeal and enthusiasm than I might have had if I had simply taken over a business. Also, it was one of my great lifetime experiences, to start my own company and have the thrill of success. I would not have had that if he had sold me his company."

Whether your exile comes as a shock or you suspect, as Jung put it, that it is an inner situation that only appears to be fate, realize that good things can come of it. No matter what its source, exile is a crucible that will force you off the couch and into the wilderness, where you can reinvent yourself.

37
Prepare an Exit Strategy

To people in the prime of life—whether twenty-five or sixty-five—retirement may seem as distant as the Promised Land. That can be a dangerous attitude if you care about the survival of your organization. When Moses died at the ripe old age of 120, he had been preparing an exit strategy for many years. In Deuteronomy, he spells it out. "I can no longer be active," he tells the Children of Israel, who have assembled at the Jordan River, at the border of the Promised Land. "Moreover, the Lord has said to me, 'You shall not go across yonder Jordan' ... Joshua is the one who shall cross before you, as the Lord has spoken....

"Then Moses called Joshua and said to him in the sight of all Israel: 'Be strong and resolute, for it is you who shall go with these people into the land that the

Lord swore to their fathers to give them ... and the Lord Himself will go before you. He will be with you.'"

Moses didn't start looking for a successor at age 119. He had singled out Joshua thirty-eight years earlier, when the young man returned from a scouting expedition to Canaan. Of the twelve men Moses sent to scout, only two, Joshua and Caleb, felt confident that they could conquer the territory. From that time forward, Moses groomed Joshua to be the next leader of Israel. But Moses didn't limit his exit strategy to choosing a successor. He also had a plan of action in place, and he had inculcated his people with a deep sense of mission before he departed. Every business owner needs to do the same, and sooner rather than later.

"How often have we heard, 'If I should die...' As if they have a choice," says Leon Danko, founder and CEO of The Center for Family Business and an authority on family succession. According to Danko, shrewd business owners will start planning their long-term goals, including an exit strategy, while they are in their forties. The statistics on the survival of family-owned enterprises underscore his point: Fewer than thirty percent of family businesses transfer to a second generation, and just thirteen percent survive to a third generation. At the heart of the problem often lies the founder's refusal to deal with his or her inevitable departure.

The brightest businesspeople recognize that while death is unavoidable, their organization need not follow them to the grave. Michael Bloomberg is founder and CEO of Bloomberg L.P., a Wall Street multimedia firm that operates across all media fronts: on-line, wire, radio, television, and print. In his book *Bloomberg by Bloomberg,* he describes how planning an exit strategy is an ongoing process. "We insist on management depth at every position. Lack of it would leave us vulnerable when someone quits or gets hit by a truck.... Every job performance review I give my direct-report managers includes the question, 'Who's your replacement? If you don't have one now, I can't consider you for bigger things. If you don't have one the next time I ask, you may no longer be a direct-report.'"

Bloomberg has no illusions about his own vulnerability: "What happens if I die, become incapacitated, or retire? What will keep the company going, protect my estate, ensure the jobs of our employees and the service to our customers?...What have I put in place for Bloomberg *without* Bloomberg?"

Bloomberg has structured his organization so that his departure will not cause extreme distress, no matter who ultimately succeeds him. "Our clients have long-term contracts with our company. Thus, the company's revenue base is very stable, and my successor will have time to grab a comfortable hold on the wheel...our employees have a long-term participation in the firm's success. The person replacing me will have to win their confidence and respect, but at least he or she will have some time to do so."

To develop a solid plan for your company's future, you have to envision a time when you will no longer be around. "It's not a comfortable thing to do," concedes Leon Danko, but the alternative can be devastating. If you wait too long to plan an exit strategy and choose a successor, you may lose the best people for the job—including children or prized employees who get tired of waiting for a piece of the action or who develop interests in other fields.

To one degree or another, everyone who founds an organization—be it a political party, a business, a nonprofit group, or a religious congregation—faces the same dilemma Moses did: Who will be best suited to carry forth the mission? Moses' choice of Joshua offers some lessons here. First, he had many years to work with Joshua and make certain the young man was right for the job. During that period, the people saw Moses and Joshua together and knew that Joshua had

Moses' blessing. This carried a lot of spiritual and psychological weight, given the fact that *God* had chosen Moses.

Second, Moses did not pick a less intense version of himself. Joshua was his own man, with an identity and style very different from that of Moses. Moses was a prophet, nearly divine. Joshua was of the people, a warrior and natural optimist. Moses' great challenge was to teach his people to be nomads; Joshua would have to wean them from the nomadic life and teach them how to settle the land. Moses had to inspire endurance and faith; Joshua would have to inspire his men to battle. Different skills for different times— Moses knew what his people would be facing, and selected a man who could keep them in touch with the old mission and sustain it in a new setting.

Imagine yourself at 120, standing on the bank of the Jordan, surveying the future. Who is steeped in the traditions you value? Who has similar aspirations for your organization? What is your plan? If you haven't yet placed yourself on that imaginary plateau, now may be the time.

Part Three

LIVING BY THE CODE

Moses did more than free a group of slaves when he led the Children of Israel to the Promised Land: He created the ethical structure upon which the Judeo-Christian world is based. The laws Moses wrote down during his forty-year sojourn in the wilderness are the same ones we still rely on for spiritual and moral guidance. They teach us how we ought to treat one another and they set the standard for an ethical society. Just as in Moses' times, it is a standard that can be difficult to meet.

This is especially true for those in business. In wartime, when people fight for their lives, moral decisions that once seemed straightforward become slippery. At work people fight for their livelihood and the same thing happens. When your family's welfare and your own career is at stake, moral questions that are crystal clear in theory fog up quickly. It is here that Moses' wisdom can offer sanctuary.

In all, Moses set down 613 commandments that include rules for ethical living. They covered virtually every permutation of human behavior—and they still do. Part Three presents those that are most important for business people. The lessons here are more about leadership than management, more about developing a strong ethical code than about business techniques. They get tested most frequently in the realm of commerce, but they are equally dependable in every avenue of life.

38
Stand Up for Your People

MOSES PLAYS MANY ROLES THROUGHOUT THE BOOK OF Exodus: liberator, lawgiver, leader. But some of his most awe-inspiring moments occur when he places himself *between* God and the Children of Israel. Time and again, Moses intercedes on their behalf. Even when they've sinned, even when it means putting his own life on the line, Moses never flinches. His support for his people is steadfast and absolute.

His biggest showdown with God erupts over the golden calf. While Moses is on Mount Sinai receiving the tablets, God gazes down to the desert floor and spies the revelry taking place around the calf. He has just liberated the Israelites from the Egyptian den of idolatry. "Hurry down, for your people, whom you brought out of the land of Egypt, have acted basely," he orders Moses. *Your* people, He says, whom *you* have brought out of Egypt. God seems to have temporarily forgotten that the Israelites are *His* people, and that He assigned Moses this task. Enraged, the Lord disavows them for their transgression. "Now let Me be," he fumes to Moses, "that My anger may blaze forth against them and that I may destroy them, and make of you a great nation."

It's a tempting offer: Get rid of the whining and uncooperative Israelites and let God create a whole new nation out of Moses' own progeny. But Moses instantly rushes to the Israelites' defense: "Let not Your anger, O Lord, blaze forth against Your people," he implores, and soon he has talked God out of His fury.

Later, when Moses is back on Mount Sinai for a second set of tablets, he clarifies his position once more. "Alas, this people is guilty of a great sin in making for themselves a god of gold," he concedes. "Now, if You will forgive their sin [well and good]; but if not, erase me from the record which you have written!" The people may have sinned, but their sin doesn't warrant their complete destruction. *If you erase them, erase me.*

God backs down in the face of Moses' commitment. "He who has sinned against Me, him only will I erase from My record," He demurs. The Children of

Israel who remained faithful to God are spared, and the nation survives.

Only Moses could have done this for the Israelites. If you are the leader, you alone can speak up for your people. That's the high price of leadership, at least for those who aspire to be great leaders. Plenty of people don't. They are the good-time leaders, taking the fat of the land when times are flush and bailing out when the economy slides or disaster strikes.

In recent years, one man made minor history simply by honoring his obligation to his workers. Aaron Feuerstein's family has owned and operated Malden Mills in Lawrence, Massachusetts, since 1906. Located in the center of town, the company employs 1,400 people. Just before Christmas in 1995, the mills burned down. What seventy-year-old Feuerstein did next was, for this day and age, unthinkable: He rebuilt.

Feuerstein's immediate reaction to the fire was to give all his workers a $275 Christmas bonus and announce that they'd receive full pay and benefits for ninety days. Although his legal and financial advisors warned him against it, he then decided to rebuild on the same spot where the mills had stood for nearly a century.

"Once you break the workers' trust, I don't think you ever get it back," Feuerstein told a reporter from the *Los*

Angeles Times. "You'll never get the quality you need. Once you treat them like a cuttable expense, instead of your most important asset, you won't recover."

Within a year of the disaster, the company had risen from the ashes. A new, state-of-the-art building was nearly complete, and a thousand employees were back at work; most of the remaining four hundred would soon follow. Widespread media attention had reaped Feuerstein millions of dollars' worth of free publicity, and production of the company's mainstays, Polartec and Polarfleece, was back where it had been before the fire.

"Everything I did after the fire was in keeping with the ethical standards I've tried to maintain my entire life," Feuerstein told the *Times,* "so it's surprising we've gotten so much attention." Mill worker Paulino Morales offered this comment: "Yeah, Mr. A [as they call Feuerstein] keeps his promises. He's someone you can trust to do well by you. But why should that be unusual for a CEO?"

Most of us will never have to deal with our enterprise burning down. Other devastating situations, such as upper management's decision to take production offshore, may be out of our hands. But on a more immediate level, we can promise our personal commitment to our employees' welfare. Even if they make mistakes, as the Children of Israel did with the golden calf, they deserve our loyalty. We all make mistakes, and we'd all prefer to be judged not by our most recent failing but by our overall performance.

When I spoke with Western International Media's Dennis Holt and Michael Kassan, they offered some revealing observations about their company's philosophy. "The importance of loyalty can't ever be stressed strongly enough," said Kassan. Acknowledging Holt's reputation as an extremely hard worker who expects the same from his staff, Kassan continued, "If an employee came in and said, 'Look, I'm going to take off Thursday and Friday because I want to play golf,' that would make Dennis crazy. But if the employee came in and said, 'My mother is sick,' Dennis would say, 'Take all the time off you need to help her, and let me know how the company can help you.'"

With few exceptions, there is no longer such a thing as thirty-year job security with assured retirement and a gold watch at the end of it all. No one can guarantee the fate of a company or an industry. Your commitment to your employees' well-being is the only security they have. Make that commitment, and they'll return the favor. "There isn't anything Mr. A could ask us that we wouldn't do," reported Malden Mills worker Angel Aponte. "I even heard one of the guys say he'd take a bullet for Mr. A."

Moses didn't always love the Children of Israel, but when he agreed to be their champion, he committed himself one hundred percent. They were, in good times and bad, "his people." You may not have the resources to rebuild a mill or face down God, but if you stand up for your people, they'll return the loyalty and effort many times over.

39
Make Your Staff into Believers

Every good manager needs to know how to balance not merely the budget or production schedule but also the big issues: beliefs versus reality. You need to believe in your company's product, your staff, and your skills, but the reality is that no matter how strong your position, everything could change next year. Ask anyone who works for a bank or an aircraft manufacturer.

Your staff is well aware of the uncertainty all around us. Yet your success depends on their morale—you must inspire them to believe in the company's future despite the stories they may hear about mergers, downsizing, and overseas competition. Moses, too, had to balance belief against reality and spur his people on in the face of terrible uncertainty.

They stood at the edge of the Sea of Reeds, the Egyptian army at their back, the shimmering expanse of water before them. Seeing the line of troops and charioteers materializing on the horizon, the Hebrews turned to Moses and cried, "Was it for want of graves in Egypt that you brought us to die in the wilderness? What have you done to us, taking us out of Egypt?"

"Have no fear, " said Moses, "The Lord will battle for you."

But God would have none of that. "Why do you cry out to me?" he demanded of Moses. "Tell the Israelites to go forward."

At that moment, their faith was put to the ultimate test. Those who really believed walked into the water. Commentaries tell us that the water did not part like a wall for the Hebrews at first. They walked in up to their necks, their chins, their mouths, before the water finally split. They moved forward as a body of faith.

The parting of the Sea of Reeds is one of the Bible's most astounding miracles. Scholars have long pondered this great event, and nearly all of them now agree that the Israelites did not cross the Red Sea, as is commonly assumed, but the Sea of Reeds, which was probably more marsh than sea. Moses no doubt knew the water was shallow; he realized that some of his people might drown but had faith that most would get through. He believed that God had not brought the Hebrews this far only to let them perish.

The dry desert winds that blow across the Sinai Peninsula sometimes sweep the water from parts of the Sea of Reeds, and this is what must have happened as Moses led the Children of Israel across. Just as they were reaching the far shore, the Egyptians plunged in after them. Weighed down with their armor, weapons, and chariots, Pharaoh's army sank deep into the marsh. The winds died down, the water returned. Shallow though it was, it was enough to drown the Egyptians—few people in ancient times could swim.

Whether we ascribe the events at the Sea of Reeds entirely to God's hand or give partial credit to Moses' timing, it was a miracle just the same. One miracle was that God chose that moment to cause the winds to rise. The other miracle is that the people believed enough to move forward.

In your business, belief is all-important. If your employees believe in the company, they won't be daunted by risks or rumors. When the armies are approaching, they'll be willing to move forward into uncertain waters.

A good manager infuses his or her staff with belief in the company's product and goals as well as the value of their individual jobs. But it's even more crucial to make sure your staff can find some aspect of the *company itself* to believe in. For nonprofit organizations committed to social causes, this is relatively easy. But most businesses don't make the world a better place or a worse one; they're just a cog in the economic wheel. To get your employees to align themselves on a deeper level, the company must step beyond the world of commerce and become involved with the community.

A few years ago I learned firsthand how a talented manager can take action for a good cause. At a charitable event, I found myself sitting next to a man named Mickey Weiss, who had grown up during the Depression and made a fortune in the produce business. As the meal ended, the two of us watched the waiters clear the buffets, carting off hundreds of pounds of untouched food. "All that waste," he mused. "By tomorrow it'll be no good."

He proceeded to tell me about a program he had started at the Los Angeles Wholesale Produce Market, where he had worked for many years importing mushrooms. One day, while walking to his loading docks, Weiss had passed an encampment of homeless people. Several blocks later, he saw two-hundred pallets of fresh strawberries about to be dumped. Because there were a few decayed berries in the flats, the County

Department of Agriculture had deemed them "edible but not salable." "Why are we throwing away berries when eight blocks away people are frying stale bread over open fires?" Weiss wondered.

In the months that followed, Mickey Weiss created a distribution center to give the excess produce to charities throughout Los Angeles. Although wholesalers had occasionally donated produce prior to Weiss's involvement, there had never been a single, centralized location for charities to collect the food. Instead, they had to drive from dock to dock, gathering what they could. Weiss organized the produce managers, dockworkers, and high school volunteers to help him provide "one-stop shopping" for the charities.

Within two years, Mickey Weiss's Charitable Distribution Facility was donating more than forty-four thousand meals a day to four hundred charities. In 1989, President George Bush presented him with an "End Hunger Award," citing Weiss's "vision, initiative, and leadership in the effort to achieve a world without hunger."

One of the reasons Mickey Weiss was able to act so decisively was that he was in the food business—he knew what sort of produce was available and how long it would stay fresh. In your own company, there may be similar opportunities to act. Are there supplies or services you could offer local schools, shelters, libraries, or community centers? Could your business provide special training to high school students?

If you can't think of anything specific your business can offer, there are still plenty of ways to get involved. Your company could pick one school to support, via scholarships or a tutoring program. You and your staff could take part in local youth programs, neighborhood tree plantings, or walks for cancer on behalf of the organization. Encourage all your employees to volunteer, and if possible, arrange for one or two workdays a year to be devoted to these events. The company that is willing to sacrifice man-hours is making a powerful statement about its commitment to the community.

Faith affects the physical universe; faith makes things happen. It's been documented that people who pray tend to recover from illnesses faster, and that doctors who pray for their patients have more success with them. Whatever crises may erupt within your business, if your staff believes in your company, their faith may be the miracle that gets you through.

40
Stand Behind
Your Decisions

WHEN MOSES FIRST ASKED PHARAOH TO LET THE Israelites go, the Egyptian ruler reacted with anger and disdain. Not only did he refuse to free the slaves, he doubled their workload. "Let heavier work be laid upon the men," he fumed to his taskmasters, and to the Israelites, "You are shirkers, shirkers!...Be off now to your work! No straw shall be issued to you, but you shall produce your quota of bricks!" Thus the slaves found themselves in worse straits than they had been before Moses made his demand. The foremen of the Israelites begged Pharaoh to reduce their burden, to no avail. As the discouraged foremen left Pharaoh's presence, "they came upon Moses and Aaron standing in their path, and they said to them, 'May the Lord look upon you and punish you for making us loathsome to Pharaoh and his courtiers—putting a sword in their hands to slay us.'" In other words, "Don't do us any more favors!"

The Children of Israel cursed Moses for trying to set them free, even though they would ultimately benefit from his efforts. They didn't see the long-term goal that Moses saw, only the immediate, unpleasant consequences of his decision to take on Pharaoh. Moses forged ahead despite the grumbling of people who didn't understand the big picture and had to suffer as a result of his actions. He did what he could to help them, but he remained resolute in his commitment to God's plan.

Strong managers must be prepared to make decisions that will be painful for some people, at least in the short term. In Moses' case, the decision to rebel against Egyptian rule led to harsher conditions for his people until they were finally released. In many companies, managers must make decisions that result in cutbacks, layoffs, or abrupt product changes. The general population, both inside and outside the company, usually won't understand the decision. But to succeed in the long run, a manager must remain fearless in the face of public disapproval.

According to Sir Adrian Cadbury, being able to make unpopular decisions is also a key aspect of *ethical* leadership. Cadbury is head of Cadbury Schwepps PLC, one of the world's largest food and beverage companies. He felt strongly enough about the topic to pen an essay on it, published in the *Harvard Business Review* in September 1987. In the article, entitled "Ethical Managers Make Their Own Rules," Cadbury pointed out that "the company which takes drastic action in order to survive is more likely to be criticized publicly than the one which fails to grasp the nettle and gradually but inexorably declines. There is always a temptation to postpone difficult decisions, but it is not in society's interest that hard choices should be evaded because of public clamor."

Seeking freedom from Egypt might seem like an obvious choice to us now, but at the time Moses proposed the idea, many people thought he was crazy. In fact, tradition has it that most of the Israelites actually *stayed* in Egypt when Moses and his followers left. They were never heard from again, but they took the comfortable path of staying in a known slavery instead of risking an unknown freedom.

The managers whom we consider visionaries have been willing to endure public disdain, sometimes for years, before they see the fruits of their labor. Dennis

Holt, founder of Western International Media, told me, "When I got this idea for a media-buying entity that would give small ad agencies some muscle, I was turned down by everybody. It wasn't 'This is a good idea—keep it up.' It was 'This is stupid.' In the late 1960s, when all this started, I was a pariah because I did something that changed the paradigm. But you have to persevere and never take bad people personally."

I faced a scenario several years ago that had me rereading Exodus time and again. It was 1992, and my contract had not been renewed at the congregation I had served for nearly eight years. With my late wife's encouragement, I decided to start a new kind of synagogue. Although there were many people who supported me in theory, when I actually announced that I was founding a new temple, the protests came loud and clear. "Los Angeles needs another temple like a hole in the head," was the most frequent observation. Not only were there plenty of temples in Los Angeles, a great many of them stood nearly empty on Friday nights. People just weren't coming. To the congregants who wished to keep attending my services, the thought of financially supporting the mortgage and mainte-nance on a new temple was daunting.

"Find an existing temple and we'll follow you there," my congregants urged. "Don't try to create a new temple. We don't need something new." The few who were up for the challenge insisted that we buy our own building, but I knew the expense would be prohibitive to too many people.

I persisted because I truly believed in my approach to Judaism, which encourages people to experience religion through music, drama, art, and dance. This had never been tried before in Los Angeles, and it was too unconventional an idea to graft on to an existing synagogue. The two synagogues that were geared toward the entertainment industry were far different from what I had in mind: One was like a club for people in the business, and the other was a meeting place for comedians—sort of a slapstick synagogue. My approach, with which I had been experimenting for eight or nine years, was to have serious performance artists *participate* in services keyed to themes that are related to our life experiences.

In the end I found a venue to rent through the late Stan Seiden, then the president of the theater-owning Nederlander Companies. Renting enabled us to avoid the cost of purchasing and maintaining a large structure. Temple Shalom for the Arts holds its services in an elegant, spacious Art Deco theater, ideal for our approach to worship. At first we attracted only four or five hundred members, but we quickly grew. Today, over two thousand congregants come to worship and enjoy musical performances, dramatic interpretations of Scripture, and other artistic expressions of the many talented people in our community.

As the leader of your organization, you shoulder the ultimate responsibility for reaching the goals you've set. You are also the person whose viewpoint should be broad enough to enable you to make wise decisions in a crunch, even if no one supports your plan.

Deep-ocean explorer Tommy Thompson faced just such a dilemma in the summer of 1986. Thompson was leading his team on a crucial stage of the search for the remains of the SS *Central America,* a sidewheel steamer that had sunk a hundred years earlier, taking with it twenty-one tons of California gold. Gary Kinder documented Thompson's saga in his best-seller *Ship of Gold in the Deep Blue Sea.* At this particular juncture, Thompson had hired a crew of expert underwater sonar technicians to scour an area of the Atlantic he had deemed likely to hold the lost ship. They had forty days to scan the area; then the weather would change and they would have to return their equipment. By that time they'd have a map of all the possible sites and could come back the following summer to claim the ship.

About three weeks into the search, the technical crew found what they were certain was the *Central*

America. With growing urgency, they began to pressure Thompson into abandoning the rest of the scan so they could concentrate on this one site and maybe even explore the ship that summer instead of waiting another year. Thompson refused. He had determined that he needed a map of the entire area. Kinder writes, "As tempting as it was to think that the *Central America* was already safely imaged in their computer and now lay waiting to be explored, Tommy wanted to avoid the mind-set of the treasure hunter, that every promising clue was the thing itself." As the days went by, the head technician intensified his pressure on Thompson, arguing that it made the most sense to send down a camera and investigate at close range.

Thompson wouldn't budge. "He didn't care how much conventional wisdom dictated otherwise, he had already confronted conventional wisdom, he was painting on a bigger canvas, and he knew other truths about the big picture," writes Kinder. They completed the entire scan, and sure enough, Thompson was right: The following summer they discovered the SS *Central America* not at the primary site but forty miles to the southwest of it, in a low-probability corner of the search map. Had they not completed the map, they would have lost another year—and perhaps lost their chance to claim the ship, since other explorers were also closing in on the site.

Just as Moses had to fight public opinion among his own people, you may one day find yourself alone with your decision, fending off protests and doomsday warnings. If your belief is strong, stand firm. It may be the only way to reach your goals.

41
Don't Compromise
with Tyranny

PHARAOH WAS THE GODHEAD OF A CULTURE THAT, AT EVERY level, reinforced the cruelty of slavery. When he decided to launch a mass genocide against the Israelites, the Bible reports, he "charged all his people, saying, 'Every boy that is born you shall throw into the Nile.'" In his book *Moses*, Jonathan Kirsch observed that this brutal decree sparked "a state-sponsored orgy of bloodletting in which every good Egyptian, soldier and civilian alike, was invited to participate as a civic duty." Moses wasn't up against a single tyrant but a culture of tyranny—a whole people who viewed the Hebrew slaves as subhuman.

When Pharaoh finally began to show signs of weakness—after his courtiers begged him to release the slaves—he offered Moses a few concessions. "Go, worship the Lord your God," he began. "Who are the ones to go?"

"We will go with our young and our old; we will go with our sons and our daughters and with our flocks and herds," replied Moses.

"No!" Pharaoh countered. "You menfolk go and worship the Lord."

But Moses wasn't about to make a deal. The Egyptians couldn't be trusted to treat the women and children well while the men were away, nor did Moses want a brief respite from slavery. He wanted absolute freedom for every man, woman, and child. He would not compromise with tyranny.

Just as Pharaoh represented a culture of cruelty, modern tyrants, whether they are dictators or taskmasters, feed off a power base of "civilians" who quietly support their actions. In the 1930s it wasn't just Hitler who decimated the Jews, but a nation full of willing citizens bred on a deeper anti-Semitism that resonated throughout Europe. Daniel Goldhagen, in his book *Hitler's Willing Executioners,* points to the widespread complicity of an entire nation in genocide, as it was whipped into a frenzy of religious hatred. When you refuse to compromise with tyranny you must recognize, as Moses did, that you are dealing with more than one person. It's rarely a matter of standing up to a single bully with everyone waiting in the wings to help. On the contrary, you may find yourself confronting your coworkers, neighbors, even your "friends," with no one to back you up.

We don't have to look as far back as Moses to find men and women willing to stand alone against tyranny. They exist in every century. In 1998 I invited the children of some extraordinary individuals to my temple on Yom Kippur Eve as we commemorated "Righteous and Honorable Diplomats" of World War II. These diplomats, none of them Jewish, hailed from Switzerland, Portugal, Japan, Sweden, Holland, China, the Vatican, the United States, and Germany. Against specific orders from their superiors, they each issued visas to Jewish refugees fleeing the Nazi regime. Unlike the Nazi officials who at the Nuremberg trials claimed only to be following orders, these humble diplomats stood against injustice to save lives. Collectively, the Righteous Diplomats rescued more than 250,000 Jews from the Nazis. Their stories can inspire us to fight our own small battles—to take an unpopular position at work, to speak up at the school board meeting, to question the rules and, if necessary, break them.

One man's tale in particular struck a chord with me, perhaps because he saw his duty so clearly and paid so high a price for his compassion. In 1938, a Catholic diplomat, Aristides de Sousa Mendes of Portugal, was appointed consul general in Bordeaux, France. The next year, following the Nazi invasion of several European nations, thousands of Jewish refugees poured into Bordeaux. Portugal was a neutral state, so de Sousa was deluged with requests for visas. If they could get to Portugal, the refugees could book passage to the United States, Canada, South America, or Palestine, far from the Nazis' reach. But within months, Portugal's foreign ministry announced a new policy: Consuls could not issue visas without prior permission. More to the point, Jews and other refugees "expelled from countries of their nationality" were to be denied entrance into Portugal.

Six months later, de Sousa faced his moral crisis. Germany invaded France on May 10, 1940, and thousands more Jews arrived in Bordeaux imploring him for visas. He wrote letters requesting the Portuguese government to relent, but got no response. De Sousa knew the refugees would be deported to concentration camps if they remained in France. After three days agonizing over his dilemma, still hearing no word from his superiors, de Sousa made up his mind to act.

"I cannot allow these people to die," he declared. "Many are Jews and our Constitution says that the religion or the politics of a foreigner shall not be used to deny him refuge in Portugal. I have decided to follow this principle. I am going to issue [a visa] to anyone who asks for it." Then de Sousa called together his staff and his two eldest sons, and they set to work stamping visas round the clock. In three days—June 17 to June 19, 1940—they issued thirty thousand visas. One of the sons, Juan Paul Abranches, brought tears to our eyes as he described the frantic effort.

By July, thousands of Jews had arrived in Portugal bearing de Sousa's visas. From there, they were able to escape Europe. Realizing what de Sousa had done, the Foreign Office demanded that he return to Portugal immediately. On his way home, de Sousa stopped in Bayonne, ordered the vice consul there to issue visas to several thousand more refugees, and personally escorted them across the border to Spain. Like Moses, the consuls held out their staff of immunity so the refugees could reach safety.

Portugal acted swiftly to punish de Sousa for his insubordination. He was dismissed and stripped of his rank, salary, and pension. In battling the dismissal, legal fees were paid by selling the family home. Although the Jewish community offered their assistance in the years that followed, de Sousa never convinced the Portuguese government to reverse their decision and readmit him to the diplomatic service. He died in 1954 in a hospital for the poor. It wasn't until 1987 that de Sousa was recognized as a hero in his own country. He has since received Portugal's Order of Liberty as well as its Gran Cross of the Order of Christ, and has been posthumously reinstated in the foreign service as an ambassador.

De Sousa wasn't shooting German soldiers or flying missions over the Rhineland. Those are heroic acts, but in de Sousa's story we find something closer to the kinds of moral dilemmas we face in peacetime. He had to break ranks with his own countrymen and endure their rejection in order to obey his conscience. To him, the choice was clear: "I would rather be with God against man than with man against God," he said.

Tyranny, says Webster's, is an "oppressive force." The force of the status quo—the silent pressure not to rock the boat—is the tyranny we most often face at the close of the twentieth century. We rarely battle "enemies" but we do encounter people who tolerate discrimination, unsafe working conditions, projects that threaten the environment, policies that cheat clients. By remembering heroes such as Aristides de Sousa Mendes, we can find the courage to speak out against these wrongs—to be with God, even if it means being against the crowd.

42
Defend Justice,
but Not for the Reward

It would be hard to name a leader who was less enthusiastic about leading than Moses when he first encountered God at the burning bush. Hiding his face in fear, he listed all his drawbacks and begged the Lord to choose someone else for the job. But Moses had one qualification that outweighed all of his flaws: He was passionately committed to justice. Throughout his life, he was the one who stepped in, stopped the fight, and took a stand when no one else would.

The Bible tells us that when he was grown, Moses left the palace grounds where he had been raised and "went out to his people and looked on their burdens; and he saw an Egyptian beating a Hebrew, one of his people. He looked this way and that, and seeing no one he slew the Egyptian and hid him in the sand," thus saving the Hebrew from the Egyptian's brutal blows.

Moses instinctively defended the underdog, although the fact that he "looked this way and that" shows he was aware there might be a price to pay. He learned what it was the next day, when he again walked among his people. This time he saw one Hebrew beating another. "Why do you strike your fellow?" asked Moses. The Hebrew retorted, "Who made you a prince and a judge over us? Do you mean to kill me as you did the Egyptian?" Undoubtedly, the Hebrew was the same slave Moses had rescued the day before. Far from being grateful, the slave resented Moses and had obviously spread word of the killing. Soon thereafter Moses was forced to flee Egypt.

All leaders eventually learn that no good deed goes unpunished. Even Abraham Lincoln is rumored to have remarked, "I don't know why that man hates me. I never helped him." Still, as a manager you must stand against injustice every time it occurs. Expect no thanks, no glory, and no support for your actions.

In nearly every instance, you'll have a choice: Stand up for your employee or let him take the blows alone. Settle the dispute or sidestep it. Stay alert to injustices or look the other way. If you choose to speak out, your colleagues and staff may turn against you for a time, as the Hebrews turned against Moses. But do it anyway, for practical as well as ethical reasons.

Your willingness to stand against injustice will ultimately win you the one element all great leaders possess: the trust of their followers. Trust is cumulative. Doing the right thing once doesn't prove much; the only way to earn your staff's confidence is to take a stand consistently, over time, whether or not people appreciate it.

One of my congregants, a woman who had recently relocated from the Midwest, recounted a story about a former supervisor whom she greatly admired. In the small town where she'd lived, there were very few Jewish families. Her religion was never an issue until the day she told her supervisor she'd be staying home for Yom Kippur, the Jewish Day of Atonement. He gladly consented, but as soon as her coworkers got wind of her plans, the grumbling started.

"They were annoyed that I got Christmas off, yet they had to work on 'my' holiday," she told me. Her supervisor acted swiftly. "He explained to the staff how important Yom Kippur was to Jewish people, as an entire day of fasting and prayer. He made it clear that he was respecting my religious beliefs and expected them to do the same. When I returned to work after the holiday, he greeted me with a big hello. By that afternoon, the others had forgotten all about it. My boss simply wouldn't tolerate their intolerance, so they let it go.

"That was his style," she reflected. "That's probably why everyone fell into line so quickly. He was on my side in this case, but he had stood up for other people in other situations."

When it came to standing up for what's right, Moses didn't play favorites. He stood between the Egyptian taskmaster and the Hebrew slave; then he interceded between the two Hebrews. Later, when he was in exile, he defended the Midianite women at the well against a group of marauding shepherds who were harassing them. Race, gender, and religion didn't matter to Moses. If he had defended only his fellow Hebrews, he would have been committed to them, but not necessarily to justice. It was his compassion for *all* human beings that gave him the courage and energy to carry out God's plan.

As a manager, your principles must apply to everyone equally. This extends beyond your employees to your supervisors, customers, vendors, and anyone else you deal with. Waver from your commitment to justice, and the bond of trust is broken. As Moses found out, eyes are everywhere. Your actions will be discovered and discussed, praised and cursed, as his were. But because he never wavered in his stand for justice, God was able to assure Moses, "They [the Hebrews] will hearken to your voice."

43

Balance Zero Tolerance with One Hundred Percent Compassion

Much is made of Moses' compassion. Who but a greatly compassionate man would have brought the Israelites out of Egypt in the first place, let alone shepherd them through the wilderness for forty years? His compassion is especially remarkable considering how little thanks he got for it. No matter how obstinate his flock, Moses consistently defended them to the Lord, often placing his life on the line to protect them.

Still, there were times when Moses reacted in anger and used drastic measures to make sure the Children of

Israel would reach the Promised Land. There were instances when he had to allow zero tolerance for backsliders. The standout example is when he came down from Mount Sinai, only to find the people reveling before a golden calf.

Moses was high on the cloudy mountainside when God alerted him that the Israelites had disobeyed Him and were now worshiping a graven image. The Lord threatened to destroy the revelers, but Moses talked Him out of it by reminding him how the Egyptians might react to such a massacre: "Let not the Egyptians say, 'It was with evil intent that He delivered them, only to kill them off in the mountains.'"

But Moses himself was not prepared for what he found at the foot of Mount Sinai. The Israelites had run wild, dancing, having orgies, and indulging in every act the Lord had specifically forbidden. Aaron feebly explained that the people had demanded an idol to worship in Moses' absence, so he told them to hand over their gold: "I hurled it into the fire and out came this calf!"

"Moses saw that the people were out of control—since Aaron had let them get out of control—so that they were a menace to any who might oppose them. Moses stood up in the gate and said, 'Whoever is for the Lord, come here!' And all the Levites rallied to him."

The moment of zero tolerance had arrived. The revelers had defied God and were undermining the entire group. Moses gave the Levites their orders: " 'Thus says the Lord, the God of Israel: Each of you put sword to thigh, go back and forth from gate to gate throughout the camp, and slay brother, neighbor, and kin.' The Levites did as Moses had bidden; and some three-thousand of the people fell that day."

What to make of a man who begs God to spare his people one day, and the next day orders a mass execution? Can zero tolerance coexist with one hundred percent compassion?

The significance of Moses' life, and what attracts us to him still, is that he embodied so many of the paradoxes we face today. He rightly earned his reputation for compassion, yet when the overall good of his people was threatened, he acted swiftly, even brutally. Moses' fierce commitment to God was matched only by his compassion for his people, and the two forces undoubtedly created intense turmoil within him. He wasn't always able to balance his commitment and his compassion, but he never stopped trying.

Contemporary leaders can also strive to balance commitment to company goals with compassion for their staff. You don't have to be extreme about it, offering your resignation one day, ordering mass firings the next. But you can carry out company policies, especially tough ones, as compassionately as possible.

One of the most difficult challenges today's managers face is substance abuse among employees. Workers who drink or take drugs compromise the team effort and the company's products or services. Worse, they endanger other people's lives, even if indirectly. Bus drivers and airline pilots clearly can't be allowed to work while intoxicated, but neither can the person who repairs the bus's brakes or manufactures the airplane's control panel.

No one argues with the idea of zero tolerance for substance abuse, but enforcing it can be daunting. Pulling aside a valued staffer and informing him that there will be zero tolerance for his hangover is a chore most of us would rather avoid. In good conscience, though, a manager can't ignore signs of substance abuse, just as Moses couldn't look the other way when he came off the mountain. He couldn't hang back and wait for the party to fizzle on its own, because that would signal his tacit approval of it.

I and just about every manager I know have had an employee show up for work under the influence. Some studies have shown that Americans consume sixty percent of the world's illegal drugs. Of alcoholics, ninety-five percent are employed, and forty-five percent of them hold management positions. So there's a good chance that sometime in your career, you'll need to deal with a substance abuser. The challenge is to do it compassionately.

Once you're aware of the problem, you must confront the individual, according to psychologist Edward Zerin. Dr. Zerin, who has counseled substance abusers for more than twenty years, says that employers are often the first to notice a change in someone's behavior and are the most effective in convincing the person to get help. "The assumption that you can't help them until they want to be helped is false," he claims. " 'Treatment or else' is the strongest motivational factor that exists. Research shows that folks who are forced into treatment have as good a chance at recovery as those who go willingly."

When you meet with the person, don't blame or be judgmental, advises Zerin. At the same time, don't make excuses for his behavior. The compassionate act is to offer the employee help, not an escape hatch. Because substance abusers can be out of touch with reality, be prepared to relate exactly what leads you to suspect the abuse—tardiness, jobs mishandled, and so forth. After you've presented your evidence, make sure your employee understands that you're not just worried about lost man-hours, you're concerned about his health and future. Reinforce the point by assuring him that he'll still have a job if he gets treatment.

"Leaders introduce spirituality into the human system by modeling unconditional (while still 'tough') love," writes business expert and author Carol S. Pearson. Even when laying off employees, she asserts, leaders should "take the needed action while making clear their continued regard for the human worth of the person."

Being compassionate is much more difficult than feeling pity. Compassion requires action, whereas pity often involves withholding action—for instance, letting a substance abuser have just one more chance. As Moses urged the Israelites across the barren desert, he must have cringed at the hungry cries of the children and longed to tell their parents, "Go ahead! Take your young ones back to the leeks, the melons, the fleshpots of Egypt!" But he took the long view. It was more compassionate to lead them to freedom than allow them to return to their masters' tables. He stuck to the plan—zero tolerance for those who defy God's laws—but his deep compassion sustained them through the hard times.

44
Teach People Not to Pass the Sting

ONE OF MOSES' GREATEST GIFTS WAS FORESIGHT. GUIDing the Israelites through the wilderness required his constant attention and effort, yet he still kept one eye on the future. He could anticipate a day when his people would not be nomads but settled in their own country, vulnerable to all the temptations of the Egyptian slave owners they had fled. This foresight is reflected in a remarkable event that took place right after God announced the Ten Commandments from Mount Sinai. In the very next chapter, Moses approaches Him alone and receives some ancillary rules—guidelines for living in a new society. The first of these rules? Laws for owning slaves.

It is astonishing for us to think that a population of former slaves, fresh from the whips of their overseers, would need to be educated about the treatment of slaves. Wouldn't they abhor slavery in any form? Moses knew the answer was no. On the contrary, former slaves make the harshest masters. Moses was acutely aware of the Israelites' history and the areas where they were most likely to falter. He was determined that they not, as Nobel Laureate Elias Canetti put it, "pass the sting" of their suffering on to their own brothers.

Among the Israelites, slavery was a means of making reparations. A slave was someone who had committed a crime or defaulted on a debt and had no way to repay it other than by offering his labor. In the wilderness, this form of slavery was sure to continue—there were no prisons, no other way to punish people who broke the Ten Commandments other than by casting them out of the group or stoning them to death, and not every transgression warranted such extreme measures.

Moses saw that his job would be to create laws that would support the ideals of the Ten Commandments while discouraging the Israelites from abusing people who broke those laws. Considering their history of slavery, the most likely way they'd pass the sting would be by mistreating their own slaves. With this in mind, it makes sense that the laws for owning slaves are the first that follow the Ten Commandments.

It's an extremely difficult balancing act: maintaining an organization's traditions and goals without nourishing a pass-the-sting mentality among the staff. Hazing rituals in fraternities and the military show just how strong the urge is to make others endure what you have had to suffer to become a member of the group. In the working world, too, the tendency is clear: If an intern must put in thirty-six-hour shifts her first year on a hospital staff, she's likely to want all the med students behind her to have to do the same thing, regardless of whether exhausted interns are a benefit to the patients or hospital.

In many professions, passing the sting is practically an institution. Junior associates in law firms toil over documents eighty or ninety hours a week. One woman who is a partner at a prestigious Los Angeles firm recalls complaining about her workload to a colleague after she had become a junior *partner.* He told her, "That's what the galley slaves are here for—you just keep rowing." She replied, "If I'd known when I came to this firm that I was applying for the job of galley slave, I would have asked for a lot more money." Universities are notorious for passing on the onerous task of grading papers to graduate students who work for a pittance. Meanwhile the professors, who have done their time as teaching assistants, are free to pursue their research—or have a long lunch at the faculty club.

Passing the sting is often an emotional reaction that diverts energy from the larger goals of the organization. As a manager, the surest way to keep your staff from falling into this trap is to know their history. When you understand the problems that are most likely to occur, you can create a set of rules that deals with them quickly—and sometimes circumvents the problems altogether.

One widespread example of passing the sting takes place in the realm of sexual relations. Most organizations have had their share of office romances, and for the past decade, that has sometimes lead to sexual harassment lawsuits. Some are clear-cut cases of harassment as most people understand it: a powerful boss making unwanted advances toward an underling. But many sexual harassment suits are murkier than that. Often it's impossible for anyone but the participants to know what really happened between them.

A situation that occurred in 1994 at Electrolizing, Inc., an industrial chrome-plating company located in Southern California, was typical of what happens when unhappy lovers want to pass the sting. As reported in the *Los Angeles Times,* a secretary at Electrolizing accused an office manager of sexually harassing her. When owner Susan Grant confronted the man, "He acted as if he had been betrayed and said, 'I'll see you in court.'" The secretary also ended up suing the company.

"If I had gone to court and lost, I would have been responsible for everyone's attorneys' fees," Grant said, referring to a California law designed to protect workers who otherwise couldn't afford to file a suit. Losing the case would have bankrupted the company, so Grant's lawyers advised her to settle out of court, with the condition that the two employees not bring any further complaints against her. By that time, however, the whole staff was feeling the sting of the lawsuit.

"This lawsuit affected every person here," Grant recalled. "The employees were taking sides.... When people heard through the grapevine how much money they were suing for, there was fear the company would go out of business." After a year of pep talks, therapy, and lawyers' fees, employee morale finally inched back to normal.

Four years later, another *Los Angeles Times* article revealed a surprising turn of events. A few farsighted companies had devised a way to deal with sexual harassment and office romances *before* they became lawsuits. The innovation is called an informed-consent agreement, and it is at the heart of new "date-and-tell" policies that encourage courting coworkers to tell their supervisors about the romance. The employer promises not to rebuke, transfer, or fire either one of the pair, and the couple agree not to sue the company for sexual harassment should the relationship turn sour.

The informed consent agreement, combined with standard sexual harassment policies, clears the waters. It treats employees like responsible adults rather than forcing them to sneak around like teenagers. Meanwhile, the company still offers recourse for people who are truly being sexually harassed. Finally, it discourages ex-lovers from passing the sting of their failed romance by filing sexual harassment suits.

Like the laws for owning slaves, date-and-tell policies grew out of an understanding of workplace history and, even more important, a realistic acceptance of human nature. As Jonas Salk once told me, "Wisdom is the ability to make retrospective judgments prospectively." Every business has built-in soft spots, situations that make the employees want to pass the sting. It may involve training procedures, comp time, credit sharing, vacation pay, dating policies, or any of a hundred other issues. The manager with foresight will learn the soft spots, read the existing policies, and if necessary set up new rules to discourage employees from passing the sting of their dissatisfaction on to others.

45
Banish Gossip

When Moses laid down the law, he made it clear that all forms of gossip are strictly forbidden: "You shall not be a gossipmonger among your people; you shall not stand by while your fellow's blood is shed." The Hebrew word for *gossipmonger* comes from the same root as the word for *peddler*. A habitual gossip is like a peddler, going from door to door carrying tidbits of information about others. What's the connection between tale bearing and bloodshed? Standing by while one person slanders another is the moral equivalent of standing by as he or she is physically assaulted. People who have been victimized by a gossip campaign can usually identify with this image.

Moses' law against gossip has spawned countless discussions among biblical scholars. For instance, people sometimes justify gossip by saying, "Well, it's true." The Bible takes an interesting stand on this point, specifically defining gossip as derogatory information that *is* true. Numerous parables illustrate how tale bearing can be damaging even if the bearer means no harm. In one of my favorites, a woman describes her neighbor by saying, "She always has something cooking on her stove." The statement can be taken as a compliment, implying that the neighbor is a generous hostess who always has a meal ready for guests. Or it can be taken as a slight, implying that the woman and her family are gluttons. The more diverse your staff, the more potential there is for misunderstandings such as this, since people from different cultural and socioeconomic backgrounds perceive ideas, and even words, differently.

When we gossip, we damage three people: the teller, the listener, and the target. This is true no matter what the intent. Even if the gossip is entirely positive, it can be harmful. "Have you met Tommy, Steve's partner? What a nice guy—and what a cook," you may enthuse to a coworker. Steve's sexual orientation may be neither here nor there to you, but who knows how the rest of the staff feel about it? Your idle words could cost Steve his next promotion.

Gossip is just as big a problem today as it was in Moses' time. If anything, there are more avenues for tale bearing now then there were back then. I heard an example of this recently when I had lunch with the human resources manager of a major petrochemical corporation, who relayed a harrowing story about gossip and its aftermath. Understandably, he asked that I not use the name of his company or any of the people involved.

"I had a woman sitting in my office sobbing yesterday," he told me. "She had already turned in her resignation, but when she explained her reasons to me, I begged her to reconsider." The woman had had a brief affair with a coworker. After the fling ended, the man threatened to send E-mail to everyone in the company, disclosing graphic details of their sexual relations. At first the woman brushed off his threats, but within days she began to notice smirks on the faces of a few colleagues. When she confronted one of them, he told her he had received a "very interesting" E-mail about her, and that her ex-boyfriend had promised to include photos the next time.

"She thought her only option was to leave the company," said the manager, "but I asked her, 'What makes you think he'll stop sending this stuff even after you leave? You have to stay and fight.' Of course, we fired the boyfriend immediately." Although the harm to this woman's reputation and peace of mind would be hard to undo, management made clear to everyone else that gossiping would be cause for dismissal.

While Moses didn't have to deal with gossip on the Internet, he was often the target of unkind "mumurings" in the wilderness. In one memorable instance, his own brother and sister were the tale bearers, speaking against Moses for marrying a woman of a different race: "He married a Cushite woman!" Moments after they uttered the words, the Lord called to Moses, Aaron, and Miriam, "Come out, you three, to the Tent of Meeting." After delivering a furious tongue-lashing to Moses' siblings, He departed, leaving Miriam "stricken with snow white scales." (The Bible isn't without humor: Miriam spoke ill of the dark-skinned woman, so God turned her white!) Moses prayed on his sister's behalf, "Please, God, heal her now!" The Lord relented and allowed Miriam's affliction to last only seven days, but the point was made: Don't talk about other people.

As a manager, you, like Moses, are the one most likely to suffer from the wagging tongues of employees. But gossip can undermine anyone. Don't wait until the E-mails start flying; let your staff know that in your place of business, gossip is not tolerated.

46

Be Responsible for Hazards You Create

I‌F MODERN SOCIETY ABIDED STRICTLY BY THE BIBLICAL code, a lot of lawyers would be out of work. The laws in the Bible are clear: Anyone who creates a hazardous situation is fully liable for the damage that occurs as a result. In Exodus we read, "If an ox shall gore a man or woman and he shall die, the ox shall surely be stoned...but if it was an ox that gores habitually from yesterday and the day before yesterday, and its owner had been warned but did not guard it, and it killed a man or woman, the ox shall be stoned and even its owner shall die."

The Bible is very straightforward on safety issues: If a person knows that his ox is likely to gore and he lets it out anyway, he is responsible for the damage. The health, safety, and environmental regulations put in place over the past few decades indicate that our society is finally catching up with basic biblical law: Don't create hazards for other people. If you do so knowingly, you must pay the price.

When new parents baby-proof their house, they take great pains to make sure the electrical outlets are covered and the Clorox and Drano are on shelves that have safety latches and are out of the baby's reach. As a manager, you need to broaden that attitude to include all those who spend the bulk of their day in your "home." Governments and big corporations may indulge in legal battles over their responsibility for the dangers of tobacco, DES, leaky fuel tanks, or plutonium dumping, but as an individual, you must hold yourself to a higher, simpler standard. If you or your company has created a hazardous situation, either knowingly or unknowingly, you have a moral responsibility to eliminate the danger once it's come to your attention.

On the job and off, we all face decisions about whether to let the ox out to gore. Even something as minor as changing the oil in your car or painting your house presents a choice: You can dispose of the oil or paint properly or illegally dump it down the sewer. My own company, Image Movement Technology, is manufacturing a moving signage system that incorporates a new synthetic paper manufactured in Asia. It's perfect for our needs, but there's one drawback—unlike inks used on regular paper, the ink used to print on synthetic paper isn't biodegradable and may require special recycling. This makes it much more costly to use than standard ink. I have the choice of disposing of the ink safely at greater expense or not using the product at all. Dumping the ink improperly isn't an option for me if I am to respect God's law.

Printing companies, in fact, used to be among the worst offenders when it came to hazardous waste. Danny ben Simon, owner of the Printing Studio in Venice, California, says that is changing. "The public doesn't know it, but the people who manufacture the products for the printing industry spend quite a bit of money on research and development to make products that are better for the environment. We would never buy a product that was potentially hazardous, but none of our suppliers or manufacturers would think of trying to sell one to us. Now that there is an awareness of being environmentally correct, it's a big selling point." The manufacturers probably didn't opt to do all that research and development on their own, but when the printers and the public began to demand safer inks, they realized that carrying such products could boost sales. Public awareness changed the industry.

Awareness is at the heart of God's injunction not to let your ox out to gore. It isn't enough to depend on government regulations. Health and environmental regulations are usually prompted by lawsuits, which in turn are a response to longstanding hazards. In many cases, the general public knew of the hazard long before laws were enacted to protect against it. For instance, studies have found that secondhand smoke is likely to cause cancer in nonsmokers who are exposed to it. Each state has responded to this news differently, so it's often the employer who must decide whether or not to allow smoking at the workplace. Could you wait until your state passes a law before you ban smoking at your office? Legally you could, but not in the eyes of God. You know that the ox is likely to gore, so you're responsible.

No amount of government regulation can extend to every instance where you might be putting others at risk. Only your conscience can provide that sort of coverage. How far should you go in promoting workplace safety? Err on the side of caution. The ancient sages counseled, "Make a fence around the Bible," meaning, make it a little stricter than is necessary. If the laws are a bit stricter, they reasoned, people will be less likely to fall into sin. In keeping with this philosophy, some traditional Jews usher in the Sabbath earlier and observe it later than required. By extending the Sabbath, they make sure no one will accidentally violate it. Similarly, if health and safety rules are a little stricter than is absolutely necessary, your people will be that much better protected.

One of the delights of reading the Bible is the clarity of its visual imagery. It's easy to get caught up in fine legal distinctions when you face the prospect of paying damages for hazards your company may have created. But if you think about the situation in terms of the ox that was known to gore, the principles—and your moral imperatives—become clearer.

47
Treat People Fairly

LONG BEFORE OSHA AND THE EQUAL OPPORTUNITY ACT, Moses was establishing a framework of humane treatment toward employees. The Lord had already commanded His people not to kill, steal, or lie, but He gets more specific when it comes to dealing with workers. "You shall not defraud your fellow," he asserts. "The wages of a laborer shall not remain with you until morning." God is equally concerned with fair treatment of those who traditionally had no rights whatsoever: "When a man strikes the eye of his slave, male or female, and destroys it, he shall let him go free on account of his eye. If he knocks out the tooth of his slave, male or female, he shall let him go free on account of his tooth."

These laws have wide-ranging implications for every manager. "Don't hold a worker's wages overnight" can be roughly translated as "Thou shalt not miss payroll." Sometimes business owners tell themselves that their employees won't mind waiting a little while to get paid. But they do mind, and as employers we have the ethical obligation to fulfill our promises to them no matter what the personal cost. "You haven't lived until you've put a payroll on your personal American Express card," says Network One founder Skip Lane. By never missing a payroll, you set an example of integrity. Missing payroll by even one day sends your staff an alarming message, both about the stability of your company and about your respect for their work.

Treating people fairly extends far beyond meeting the payroll. Creating a safe workplace and going the extra mile when accidents occur will reap you huge dividends in employee loyalty. Dr. Howard Stern, medical director of Arco Products Company, recalls an incident when his company had the chance to prove their compassion and regard for employees: "We recently had an employee who was seriously injured when a rock shattered the windshield of his tanker truck while he was driving on the highway in Nevada. We could have had him cared for in that community, but instead we decided to fly him that day to a specialty eye clinic in Los Angeles where he could be seen by some of the best specialists in the country. He did very well and soon came back to work for us. He did not have any questions or concerns about the quality of the care and he will always know that the company cares about every one of our employees."

Participating in preventive health care programs is one way a company can show its commitment to its employees and practice "proactive" fairness. PHP Benefit Systems, an association of individual health care practitioners, has a breast health awareness program. All female members over twenty-one receive a packet containing a brochure on detecting breast cancer, a self-examination guide, a reminder bookmark, and a survey inquiring about the impact of the program. Pat Carroll, vice president of health services for PHP's commercial HMO, says that the money for the program is well spent: "The cost of mammograms and [the breast health program] is minuscule compared to the potential cost—both personal and financial—of full-blown cancer. If you can prevent one bone marrow transplant you've recouped your dollars."

A. Robert Davies, M.D., vice president and chief medical director at Nationwide Insurance Companies, echoes this sentiment. Eighty-five percent of Nationwide's employees participate in company-sponsored wellness programs. "We spend a lot of money on maintaining our computer resources, our buildings, et cetera. This is money spent to maintain our human resources."

Research has indicated that money is not the main reason people go to work. Yes, they want to get paid, but in surveys of employee motivation, pay consistently comes in around fifth on the list of reasons to work. The most valuable thing you can give your employees is the sense that they matter, that their contributions are vital to your company's success. "We don't pay high salaries here," says Skip Lane. "Instead, we're telling [our employees], 'You're building something and you are a contributor and your voice counts." As an upstart telecom company, Lane at first felt like a small fish in a very big pond. To keep his employees motivated, he says, "I knew I had to have people buy into the dream.... How did I do that? I made them more important than me."

There are thousands of state and federal regulations mandating fair treatment of employees. We're often so concerned with obeying the letter of these laws that it's easy to lose track of the spirit behind them. Ultimately, the reason to respect people, pay them fairly and promptly, take care of them when they are injured on the job, and offer them programs to keep them healthy is *not* because you want to avoid a lawsuit. It's because treating people fairly is the right thing to do.

48
Maintain Honest Weights and Measures

ACCORDING TO AN ANCIENT TRADITION, THE FIRST QUES-
tion we will be asked when we reach the next world is
not "Did you believe in God?" but "Were you honest
in your business dealings?" Whether we are selling a
service or a product, we have a moral obligation to be
scrupulously honest in all our measurements. In Leviticus we read, "You shall not make a perversion in justice, in measures of length, weight, or volume. You
shall have correct scales, correct weights, correct dry
measures, and correct liquid measures." The instructions are deceptively simple. In everyday life, this kind
of honesty requires that we overcome a wide range of
rationalizations within ourselves.

If the customer is a huge, impersonal organization, or if we feel we've been treated unfairly in some other aspect of our relationship, we may tell ourselves that deceiving the customer is downright virtuous. Vendors may reason, "This is the government—they're cheating me out of my taxes, so why shouldn't I charge them a hundred dollars for a ten-dollar hammer?" or "This is a huge corporation—what's a few dollars to them? It's nothing to them and it's a lot to me, so I'll go ahead and charge extra." We fall prey to these temptations without realizing that even if the customer pays the money, we ourselves ultimately pay the price. We pay in loss of self-respect about our own integrity, we pay in loss of sensitivity to nuances of morality, and we pay in the slowly eroding trust between ourselves and our customers.

Moshe Chaim Luzzatto, author of the ethical treatise *Path of the Just*, wrote:

> Although most people are not manifest thieves in the sense of openly confiscating their neighbors' belongings and depositing them among their own possessions, most of them get the taste of theft in the course of their business dealings by allowing themselves to gain through their neighbors' loss, saying, "Business is different." Whatever effort is

made to show the purchaser the true worth and beauty of the object is fitting and proper, but whatever is done to conceal its imperfections constitutes deceit and is forbidden.

The Bible requires merchants to clean their measures once every thirty days. Luzzatto explains that this is necessary "so that the purchasers not unknowingly get less than what they paid for and the merchant not be punished." The temptation to mislead or cheat—just slightly—is always present in business. Perhaps it is because there's a fine line between putting a positive spin on a product, which is good marketing, and implying something that is untrue. Perhaps it is because the urge to rationalize and deceive ourselves is especially strong in cases where we personally stand to gain or lose money. Whatever the reason, Moses seems to be suggesting that we try to overcome our natural self-serving inclinations by establishing objective, fair measures of the quantity of the goods we sell.

When measuring pounds of coffee or ounces of gold, you can rely on your scales (as long as you've checked them). But in service businesses, such as consulting and law, in which clients trust the service provider to keep careful track of time spent on a project, the necessity for keeping careful records is even more urgent. If a lawyer is being paid by the hour and he stops in the middle of one client's work to take a ten-minute phone call from another client, does he work ten minutes over that hour to compensate for the time he took away? Or does he say, "It was such a short call, it doesn't matter." Or "Hey, this client can afford it. So what if I charge for the whole hour?" There is a joke about a lawyer who dies at age forty and ascends for his interview at the gates of heaven. The lawyer complains, "How can you call me here so soon? I'm only forty years old!" The guardian of the gates consults his records and says, "That's surprising. According to your hourly billing records, you're ninety!" Through these laws, Moses is trying to convey that it is irrelevant whether the client can afford it, or whether the client ever finds out.

Employers can also use roundabout means of measuring time as a way of cheating their employees. "Just work overtime this week," says the boss, "and you can take extra personal time off whenever you want to!" So the employee works the extra hours without compensation. But somehow, that extra time off doesn't happen. Instead, there are more and more hours of overtime, and more vague promises of personal time off— accompanied by the employee's gradually increasing sense of being taken advantage of. If you intend to give people time off for overtime, set up a compensation formula whereby they can trade in their "comp" time for money at the end of a specified time period.

Maintaining honest weights and measures involves more than keeping an accurate set of scales. It is a mind-set of meticulous respect for the trust that your customers place in you, and for the value of the money that they are paying you. When we return to the biblical adage "Love your neighbor as yourself," the dictum about weights and measures becomes clearer. You wouldn't want to be charged for an hour's work when your lawyer actually spent part of that hour on the phone with someone else. You don't want to be misled, and neither do other people. This ethical truth is obvious, but in the competitive pressures of the marketplace, it is very difficult to follow. That is why business ethics is given so much importance in biblical law— and that is why, in the final analysis, whether you keep honest time records and use truthful product packaging may matter more to your spiritual well-being than all the ritual practice in the world.

49
Don't Place a Stumbling Block Before the Blind

MOSES BUILT THE FOUNDATION OF HIS SOCIETY BRICK BY brick, with a multitude of laws. Many of these are straightforward: "You shall not steal, nor deal falsely, nor lie to one another.... You shall not oppress your neighbor or rob him." But there are other, less obvious rules that have much to teach us as well. One of these is, "You shall not curse the deaf, and you shall not place a stumbling block before the blind, but you shall fear your God: I am the Lord." While most of us don't go to work each morning plotting to curse the deaf and trip the blind, if we stop and think for a moment, the application in everyday life becomes clear.

Cursing the deaf can be belittling an employee who's not around to defend himself, or expressing exasperation over someone's efforts or appearance when you know there is nothing she can do to improve. Cursing the deaf is more than just gossiping, which is bad enough in itself. When you curse the deaf you disparage someone who is not only unaware of your ill will but unable to change that particular characteristic, even if you told her to her face. The harm you do the other person is immeasurable, even if she is "deaf" to your bad-mouthing. You are demonstrating disrespect for her, and that can have a negative ripple effect throughout the organization.

What about putting stumbling blocks before the blind? Giving bad advice to someone who is not equipped to make a decision is certainly putting a stumbling block in his path. When a salesperson advises a customer to buy a computer with expensive, complex features that the person will never use, he is placing a stumbling block in that person's path. Tobacco companies that intentionally lace cigarettes with nicotine when they know that nicotine is both physically addictive and harmful are also placing stumbling blocks before the blind.

As a manager and a colleague, you face multiple opportunities every day to curse the deaf or place a stumbling block before the blind, figuratively speaking. When you think in terms of literally putting an obstacle in front of a person who can't see it and waiting for him to trip, the meanness of the act is plain. But in daily practice, issues often blur. You know that your assistant is not really ready to prepare and deliver a sales presentation alone, but you tell her, "Go ahead! I'm sure you'll do fine. You don't need me." You have key information that a colleague is unaware of and you wait until he has given his opinion at a meeting before you present the data that would have changed his views, had he known about it. You promote a person to a supervisory position but fail to provide any training in supervisory skills. The possibilities are endless.

In the case of cursing the deaf, the person who's being cursed may suffer great emotional distress when your words finally reach her ears, as they inevitably will. In the case of the stumbling block, the ignorant—figuratively blind—person often falls and really gets hurt. People who believed nicotine was harmless really did become addicted and die of lung cancer. People urged into jobs for which they are unprepared really do fail and take the blame for it in their careers. Clients persuaded to buy services, products, or property they don't understand and can't afford really do go bankrupt. In each case you can lounge back and say "caveat emptor"—it was the blind person's own fault that he tripped.

The laws of Moses prohibit this type of action because it undermines a fundamental tenet of human society: respect for all people, regardless of their handicaps and limitations. Moses was nothing if not realistic. He didn't trust people to refrain from such behavior simply because it is morally wrong. That's why he added the phrase "You shall fear God" after these admonitions. We cannot treat one another with passive cruelty and expect to emerge unharmed. In the short term, we harm ourselves just by being people who behave that way, and by becoming known as people who behave that way. According to the Bible, some cosmic consequence ensues as well. If reading the Bible does anything for us, it provides us with vivid metaphors for situations that may at first seem fuzzy. Once in your mind, these metaphors have a habit of sticking there. Don't curse the deaf or place a stumbling block before the blind—now that you've read them, you'll surely recognize these situations more easily.

50
Remember the
Small Gestures

Alone and friendless, Moses entered the wilderness
of Midian a wanted man, a death sentence on his
head for slaying the Egyptian taskmaster. Soon he
found himself pulled into a local drama: "The priest
of Midian had seven daughters. They came to draw
water and filled the troughs to water their father's
flock; but shepherds came and drove them off. Moses
rose to their defense, and he watered their flock.
When they returned to their father Reuel [Jethro], he
said, 'How is it that you have come back so soon
today?' They answered, 'An Egyptian rescued us from
the shepherds; he even drew water for us and watered
the flock.' He said to his daughters, 'Where is he

then? Why did you leave the man? Ask him in to break bread.'"

Moses ran to Midian, fleeing for his life. He did a favor for seven young women whom he did not know. In gratitude, their father invited him to share a meal. Moses eventually married Zipporah, one of Jethro's daughters. Small gestures of concern for another person's welfare, or of simple hospitality, have an enormous impact on people's sense of connection with you.

Life is lived in the small gestures—the door held open for another person, the glass of water offered to a visitor to your office, the ten seconds it takes to ask a secretary if her child has recovered from the flu. Be on the lookout for opportunities to practice these "random acts of kindness" on the people you work with.

Even small habits of hospitality can have a profound impact on company culture. Elizabeth Danziger, president of Worktalk Communications Consulting in Venice, California, recalls teaching a writing class at the corporate headquarters of T.J. Lipton, the tea makers. "Everyone was paying close attention to the training. At ten-fifteen in the morning, the participants suddenly started glancing at one another and the door. I asked them what was happening. One person replied,

'It's the tea cart. Every day the tea cart comes down the hall at about this time. No one wants to miss their tea break.' I called a break, and we all went out into the hall to watch for the cart. There was a delicate ringing of a bell, followed by the sight of a kindly lady pushing a cart that contained iced tea, hot tea, and home-made cookies. People flocked from their offices to say hello to one another and enjoy their morning tea break. By creating this 'tea ritual' for all employees, Lipton had created a sense of home for them and had given everyone a chance to connect."

As business communication becomes ever more electronic, gestures of human warmth will take on even greater significance. If an employee receives forty E-mails and twenty-five voice-mails a day, all pouring information into his already overloaded mind, consider the impact it will have if you send him a handwritten note that says, "I know how hard you're working on this project. Thank you." If you are in the same building, take a moment to speak to the person face-to-face, even if you could have handled the conversation electronically. "Face time" is becoming a precious commodity.

Barry Sternlicht, chairman and CEO of Starwood Hotels and Resorts, told me recently of his plans to make his hotel rooms even more appealing to guests. How was he going to do this? By buying higher quality pillows. "That's one thing everyone remembers—the way the pillow felt when they lay their head on it. It makes all the difference in a good night's sleep. For a few dollars more per pillow, I can provide that. Details like that are what makes a hotel great."

The little things you do to show consideration for your employees will also contribute to their loyalty. Elizabeth Brenner, a small-business owner in California, recalls a company where she worked as an office assistant many years ago. "It was a family-owned Japanese trading company with about twenty employees. Every morning the owner's wife would put up a huge pot of rice on the rice cooker in the company kitchen. And every day at lunch, the owner would formally dish out a bowl of white rice to all his employees. People might have their sandwiches and fast-food hamburgers, too, but everyone took a little of that rice. I felt it created an old-fashioned civility, as though the owner wanted to demonstrate that he felt it was his duty to feed his employees."

When Abraham had guests in the desert, he washed their feet for them and slaughtered his best lamb to serve them dinner. Moses watered the flock of seven young women who were strangers to him. As a contemporary manager, you have it easy—no feet to wash, no flocks to water. But each personal interaction with an employee, a colleague, or a customer is an opportunity to demonstrate your character through the small gestures you choose to make.

CONCLUSION
From Words to Deeds

OVER THE PAST DECADE THERE HAS BEEN AN INCREAS-
ingly holistic approach to business management. Com-
partmentalizing is out, looking for organic solutions is
in; the autocratic structure of leadership is out, team
building and creative problem-solving are in. Sadly,
when it comes to ethics in the workplace, things have
not evolved so quickly. Too many of us still believe we
can be cutthroat six days a week and save our souls on
the seventh. In truth, the deal we make on Tuesday car-
ries as much moral weight as the prayers we recite on
Saturday or Sunday.

The business world and the moral world are one
and the same. Management involves taking actions, and
any time we take an action at work there are both business and moral consequences. According to Dr. Burt
Visotzky, a professor at New York's Jewish Theologi-
cal Seminary, "The Bible is all about business. In Exodus, people step out of the family, forming a corporate
identity. A lot of negotiation goes on. Abraham negotiates with God, with Pharaoh; Moses negotiates with

God, with the people. Most importantly, he learns how to delegate authority. You need an ethos wherein you consider ethical practice part of your obligation to shareholders."

Through Moses, God gave us not ten but 613 "laws of human kindness"—the commandments contained in the first five books of the Bible. If we are to evolve, we must learn to embrace these laws and balance business with ethics. The story of Moses shows us some of the ways we can achieve this. His formula for leading people through difficult times can be summarized in ten words:

- ◆ accept
- ◆ assess
- ◆ connect
- ◆ deliver
- ◆ persevere
- ◆ solve
- ◆ search
- ◆ enforce
- ◆ endow
- ◆ depart

Accept. Accept the role of leadership, even if you're reluctant, unwilling, and feel unequipped for the job.

Accept the fact that someone has to lead, and it might as well be you. The story of Moses shows us that sometimes the person who appears least likely to be a leader can step forward and lead magnificently. Often the people who don't see themselves as natural leaders are the ones with the most innovative ideas. Accept the role of leadership, and know that no matter what your background, you have something valuable to contribute.

Assess. Assess the situation you're about to enter. Moses had to assess the Egyptians, the Hebrews, the environment, the terrain, and the history of Egyptian culture. Likewise, a new manager must assess the staff, management, surroundings, corporate history, and goals of the organization. Even though circumstances may change dramatically, it's vital to familiarize yourself with the terrain as it exists right now. There is also a moral element to assessment: What impact is the organization having on its employees, the community, and the environment? A crucial part of your job as manager is to balance the financial goals of the company with its larger role in society.

Connect. Moses made a connection with God, and that connection was the driving force throughout his life. As a manager, you have to establish a connection with the objectives of the company. If you are detached from the organization's goals and approach the job as if you're just a cog in the big machine, you won't be able to sustain your enthusiasm, and your mission will become much harder.

You'll also need to connect with the people around you. The bond Moses established with the Children of Israel was essential to his success. Even though biblical commentators often call Moses "God's Man," he was also a man of the people. Moses transmitted God's words to the Israelites, and it was the Israelites who struggled for survival alongside Moses. In your daily work, you're not going to be dealing solely with corporate mission statements. You're going to be dealing with people, and your connection with them is all-important.

Deliver. The results you deliver will earn you the respect of your colleagues. In the Bible, however, the word *deliver* takes on a more complex meaning. Moses didn't simply deliver God's message to the people, he also delivered their pleas and prayers to God. Furthermore, he was the instrument of their deliverance from bondage. As a manager, you are a two-way conduit between your team and upper management. You must not only deliver the goods, you must deliver your employees from unjust treatment, unsafe conditions, and unreasonable demands. Deliver on the goals you set for the company, but always weigh those goals against the welfare of your staff.

Persevere. Moses waited through ten plagues for Pharaoh to grant the Children of Israel their freedom—and many commentators believe that the plagues occurred over a stretch of years, not weeks or months. Then he guided his people for forty years in the wilderness, enduring their backsliding yet never doubting that they would eventually reach the Promised Land. Moses' perseverance made their success possible. In the same way, you must demonstrate to your staff that no matter what obstacles arise, you will be there for them. Do this simply by coming in every day on time and steadily working through good years and bad. The more time you spend at the company, and the more troubling times you weather, the stronger and more resolute you and your team will become.

Solve. Being in business is all about solving problems. Problems will never go away, and if you put them on the back burner they'll only resurface later. Paul

Hawkin, founder of Smith & Hawkin, wrote that for years he was like a greyhound chasing the rabbit of permanent solutions. Then, one afternoon, he had a revelation: "I would always have problems. In fact, problems signify that the business is in a rapid learning phase." Moses was continually solving problems: supplying food and water for his people, teaching them survival skills, navigating their journey, grooming them to settle the Promised Land. If he couldn't solve a problem himself, he found someone who could help him. Although his tasks were often overwhelming, he didn't give up. He solved each problem as it arose, and then turned to the next one.

Search. Search out people and ideas that will help you expand your horizons. Moses absorbed information from widely diverse sources, including Pharaoh's court, where he was raised; the desert wilderness where he tended his flock; his magistrates and lieutenants; and his father-in-law, Jethro. It was his searching nature that led him to investigate the burning bush. In your own life, seek out knowledge not just from your field but from any field that seems promising: psychology, religion, literature, science. There is no single, exclusive source of knowledge. A searcher knows how to draw water from many wells, not just one.

Enforce. You, as manager, must enforce a set of rules. If you're not going to enforce them, they become meaningless. One great truth the Ten Commandments teach us is that people will try to avoid following any set of rules, even those that are fair and just. When confronted with enough temptation, now as in ancient days, people kill, steal, and commit adultery. The Ten Commandments propose a code of conduct that does not come easily to human beings, but Moses was unyielding in enforcing that code. Had he made an exception here and there, his group would have disintegrated from internal fighting. Your role as manager is to enforce your organization's policies fairly and consistently so that peace and civility can flourish in your workplace.

Endow. Moses' goal during his lifetime was not simply to bring the Israelites out of Egypt but to endow them with the knowledge they would need to flourish as a free people. He gave them a mission—to secure the Promised Land—a belief system, and practical survival skills. When contemplating your legacy, think beyond profits earned or products launched. Does your style of leadership reflect the value system you would like to see throughout the company? Are you endowing your people with a mission for the future, a set of beliefs about what your company stands for, and the practical skills they need to succeed?

Depart. Know when it is time to leave. Moses may not have been happy about being denied entrance to the Promised Land, but he realized it was time for new leadership. He had selected a successor, Joshua, many years earlier, and, at the border of Canaan, Moses publicly gave Joshua his blessing. What most concerned Moses at the end of his life was that the organization continue to thrive after he was gone.

How do you know when it's time to move on? Mo Seigal recently left the company he founded, Celestial Seasonings, after twenty-two years. According to Seigal, you can clarify your feelings by asking yourself questions such as:

- Can I find someone who can do a better job than I can?
- Can I still add value to the company?
- Am I happy? Is working here what I want, or are there other things I'd like to do?

Whether you are CEO of a large corporation or the owner of a five-person shop, these questions are equally valuable. No matter how successful you are, there will come a time to let go. If you recognize that moment, you can make the transition purposefully and enter the next phase of your life—be it another job, an entrepreneurial venture, or retirement—with optimism and energy.

Each of these ten words is a verb—an action word. A person's beliefs are meaningful only in light of his or her actions: deeds over creeds. Recall that God told Moses, "Better that My people should not believe in Me but observe My laws, than believe in Me but not observe My laws." Belief may ebb and flow, but actions are what counts. As you carry out your mission, let God's laws of human kindness guide your actions and help deliver you and those you lead to a more peaceful, more rewarding life.

BIBLICAL REFERENCES

(in order of their occurrence in each Leadership Lesson)

PART ONE: *Delivering the Message*

1. Allow Others to Recognize Your Strengths and Recognize the Strengths in Others—Exodus 3–4.

2. Cultivate the Inner Qualities of Leadership—Exodus 3:11.

3. Speak to People on Their Own Level, and Make It Personal—Numbers 12:8; Exodus 20:15–16, 19:25; Deuteronomy 32:46–47.

4. Ask for What You Want—Exodus 3:19; Matthew 7:7–8.

5. Let Them Know Your Ways—Exodus 33:12–13.

6. Use a Mission Statement as Your Ten Commandments—Exodus 24:3–7.

7. Realize That Faith Must Be Renewed—Exodus 4:1, 30, 15:1, 17:3–4; Deuteronomy 29:4.

8. Negotiate Face-to-Face—Deuteronomy 34:10; Exodus 33:11; Numbers 12:7–8.

9. Maximize Your Second-in-Command—Exodus 4:10–16.

PART THREE: *Living by the Code*

40. Stand Behind Your Decisions—Exodus 5:9–23.

41. Don't Compromise with Tyranny—Exodus 1:22, 10:8–11.

42. Defend Justice, but Not for the Reward—Exodus 2:11–14.

43. Balance Zero Tolerance with One Hundred Percent Compassion—Exodus 32:7, 24–28.

44. Teach People Not to Pass the Sting—Exodus 21:1–11.

45. Banish Gossip—Leviticus 19:16; Numbers 12:1–13.

46. Be Responsible for Hazards You Create—Exodus 21:28.

47. Treat People Fairly—Leviticus 19:13; Exodus 21:26.

48. Maintain Honest Weights and Measures—Leviticus 18:19, 19:35.

49. Don't Place a Stumbling Block Before the Blind—Leviticus 19:14.

50. Remember the Small Gestures—Exodus 2:16–20.

BIBLIOGRAPHY

Two editions of the Bible were used as sources for this book:

Tanakh: The Holy Scriptures. The New JPS Translation According to the Traditional Hebrew Text. Philadelphia and Jerusalem: Jewish Publication Society, 1985.

The Chumash, Stone Edition. New York: Mesorah Publications, 1994.

Books

Bennis, Warren. *On Becoming a Leader.* Reading, Mass.: Perseus Books, 1989.

Bennis, Warren, and Burt Nanus. *Leaders.* New York: HarperCollins, 1997.

Bennis, Warren, with Patricia Ward Biederman. *Organizing Genius: The Secrets of Creative Collaboration.* Reading, Mass.: Addison Wesley, 1997.

Bloomberg, Michael, with Mathew Winkler. *Bloomberg by Bloomberg.* New York: John Wiley, 1997.

Bock, Emil. *Moses.* New York: Inner Traditions International, 1998.

Branden, Nathaniel. *Self-Esteem at Work.* San Francisco: Jossey Bass, 1998.

Cahill, Thomas. *The Gifts of the Jews.* New York: Doubleday, 1998.

Covey, Stephen. *Seven Habits of Highly Effective People.* New York: Simon & Schuster, 1989.

Daiches, David. *Moses: The Man and His Vision.* New York: Praeger, 1975.

Dauphinais, G. William, and Colin Price, eds. *Straight from the CEO: The World's Top Business Leaders Reveal Ideas That Every Manager Can Use.* New York: Simon & Schuster, 1998.

Dell, Michael, with Catherine Fredman. *Direct from Dell: Strategies That Revolutionized an Industry.* New York: HarperCollins, 1999.

Farson, Richard. *Management of the Absurd.* New York: Simon & Schuster, 1996.

Ginzberg, Louis, and Paul Radin. *The Legends of the Jews: Moses in the Wilderness.* Baltimore: Johns Hopkins University Press, 1998.

Ginzberg, Louis, and Henrietta Szold. *The Legends of the Jews: From Joseph to the Exodus.* Baltimore: Johns Hopkins University Press, 1998.

Goleman, Daniel. *Working with Emotional Intelligence.* New York: Bantam Books, 1998.

de Grazia, Alfred. *God's Fire.* Princeton, N.J.: Metron Publications, 1983.

Kirsch, Jonathan. *Moses: A Life.* New York: Ballantine Books, 1998.

Luzzatto, Moshe Chaim. *Path of the Just,* 2d rev. ed. Jerusalem/New York: Feldheim Publishers, 1980.

Senge, Peter M. (editor), Art Kleiner (editor), Charlotte Roberts. *The Fifth Discipline Fieldbook.* New York: Currency/Doubleday, 1994.

Silver, Daniel J. *Images of Moses.* New York: Basic Books, 1982.

Wildavsky, Aaron. *The Nursing Father: Moses as a Political Leader.* University of Alabama Press, 1984.

Newspapers and Periodicals

Atkinson, Greg. "Prince of Peach." *Seattle Times,* July 26, 1998.

Cadbury, Adrian. "Ethical Managers Make Their Own Rules." *Harvard Business Review,* September 1987.

Colloff, Pamela. "Contrition." *Texas Monthly,* August 1998.

Cook, Richard. "The Rogers Commission Failed." *The Washington Monthly,* November 1986.

"Different Worlds: More entrepreneurs are arriving with corporate expertise—good and bad; we ask three what it has meant and what they've discovered." *The Wall Street Journal,* June 6, 1998.

Ellin, Abby. "Their Business Bible Is, Well, the Bible." *New York Times,* January 17, 1999.

Evers, Tag. "A Healing Approach to Crime." *The Progressive,* September 1998.

"Following Suit: Restoring Harmony in Wake of Harassment Case." *Los Angeles Times,* November 12, 1996.

Goleman, Daniel. "What Makes a Leader?" *Harvard Business Review,* November–December 1998.

Henry, Dennis. "Family Ties: Keeping a Business in the Family." *Business 98,* December–January 1998.

Hong, Peter Y. "Diversity Driven by the Dollar." *Los Angeles Times,* May 26, 1998.

Krass, Peter. "Landed a Monopoly by Always Taking on the Impossible." *Investor's Business Daily,* July 21, 1998.

Lamb, David. "Ethics, Loyalty Are Tightly Woven at Mill." *Los Angeles Times,* December 19, 1996.

"Letting Go: Celestial Seasonings' Mo Siegal on How He Knew It Was Time to Step Down." *Inc.,* April 1999.

Lyster, Michael. "Hoops Star Chamique Holdsclaw: How She Became the Best Player in Women's College Basketball." *Investor's Business Daily.*

Morris, Nomi. "Demanding Justice." *Maclean's,* June 9, 1997.

" 'Old' Coke Back Again, But Where Will Chains Put It?" *Nation's Restaurant News,* July 7, 1985.

Pearson, Carol S. *Thinking About Business Differently* [booklet]. Aliso Viejo, Ca: InnoVisual Communications, 1998.

Prager, Joshua Harris. "Superman Transforms Spinal Research." *The Wall Street Journal*, November 18, 1996.

Prickett, Ruth. "Alive and Kicking." *People Management*, May 15, 1997.

Raspberry, William. "Not-So-Funny Business." *The Washington Post*, February 1, 1999.

Rosenthal, Andrew. "Bush Encounters Supermarket, Amazed." *New York Times*, February 5, 1992.

Silverstein, Stuart. "New Rules of Office Romance." *Los Angeles Times*, September 23, 1998.

Stettner, Morey. "7 Deadly Phrases That Undermine Managers." *Investor's Business Daily*, April 24, 1997.

Strebel, Paul. "Why Do Employees Resist Change?" *Harvard Business Review*, May–June 1996.

Torres, Vicki. "Worker Bees Take 'Bold Steps' on County Contracting." *Los Angeles Times*, September 9, 1998.

"Winner and Still Champion." *Time*, October 23, 1985.

Woodlee, Yolanda. "Mayor Acted 'Hastily'; Will Rehire Aid." *The Washington Post*, February 4, 1999.

ACKNOWLEDGMENTS

Throughout my rabbinical career and life experience there have been numerous teachers whose instruction has been of inestimable value. Their written commentaries and actions have demonstrated the vitality of the Scripture in relation to human commerce and the importance of leadership in each generation. I also wish to acknowledge the corporate CEOs and chairmen who shared their insights. In the words of the Talmud: "From all of my teachers have I grown in wisdom."

My colleague Dr. Edward Zerin and his wife, Dr. Marjory Zerin,, were helpful in assembling religious perspectives on the workplace, as was Elizabeth Danzinger at Worktalk Communications. My dear friend Tom Drucker at Consultants in Corporate Innovation shared valuable insights in his dealings with Fortune 500 companies. I was truly privileged to meet with Dr. Warren Bennis in the Department of Management and Organization at the University of Southern California's School of Business. All of his writings were a great source of inspiration, as was Dr. Nathaniel Branden's *Self-Esteem at*

Work. A special round of thanks goes out to my coauthor, Lynette Padwa, whose gift for clarity and persistence in the face of numerous congregational life-cycle events was so helpful. My literary agent, Betsy Amster, was a great asset in facilitating this process. Senior editor Mitchell Ivers at Pocket Books demonstrated vast expertise and nurturing guidance, and I am most appreciative of his encouragement. At my office, I want to thank Harvey Morgenbesser for his help. Lastly, I wish to thank my patient family—Ellen, Jennifer, Sarah, and Jonathan—for their understanding and support.